T0198616

Horses Happen!

Horses Happen!

✦

A Survival Guide for First-Time Horse Owners

Joanne M. Friedman

iUniverse, Inc.
New York   Bloomington

Horses Happen!

A Survival Guide for First-Time Horse Owners

iUniverse books may be ordered through booksellers or by contacting:

iUniverse
1663 Liberty Drive
Bloomington, IN 47403
www.iuniverse.com
1-800-Authors (1-800-288-4677)

ISBN: 978-1-4401-8294-5 (pbk)
ISBN: 978-1-4401-8295-2 (ebk)

Printed in the United States of America

iUniverse rev. date: 10/21/2009

Contents

How Could This
Have Happened to You?

You never really thought you would own a horse. Maybe you were nursing an unrequited childhood pony lust, or maybe your dreams centered more on fast cars and big houses. Everything changed when one day little Suzy (or Marie, or, occasionally, Tommy) took a field trip to a local horse farm. The blackmailing was insidious. There would be no appropriate bedtime, no quiet meals, and no sane conversation in the house until you put down your newspaper or turned off your computer and gave your full and earnest attention to the whiny little monster who used to be your child. "But, Mom! Dad!" you heard, *"Everybody's getting a horse but me!"*

Naturally, this statement was suspect from the get-go. Granted, you'd been a little out of touch with your child's friends, but you were pretty sure none of the neighbors' yards had sprouted grass-nibbling critters bigger than your SUV.

Still, the Good Parent voice in your head was shrieking, "Do you want all the other parents to think you can't afford to give your kid whatever her over-marketed little brain thinks she needs?" No micro-parent worth her (or his) salt would overstep this bound.

So, checkbook in hand, you hauled little Lindsay off to the nearest horse emporium, The Silver Spur Happy Trails Riding Stable (Horses For Hire and Sale, Riding Lessons by Appointment). You found yourself standing toe-to-hoof with the biggest, dustiest, homeliest monster that's ever escaped from your nightmares. Your child was hopping from foot to foot in excitement. The dealer was smiling around his chaw of nicotine-replacement gum, and someone was handing you a rope. You might as well have used it to tether yourself to the nearest flagpole, because this was the start of a wild ride.

Welcome, Fellow Traveler, to the Wild World of Horse Ownership!

"Look into my eye… You're getting sleepy…"

Part One:

On Misleading and Being Mislead

Things That Go Wrong

- The Wrong Reason

Why do you want a horse? Will a dog or a gerbil suffice to fill the need? If so, you're doing this for the wrong reason. A small child is no arbiter of common sense when it comes to a life decision as huge as this. If you truly believe a seven-year-old carrying a stuffed pony and crying into her oatmeal is capable of directing the entire family's existence for the next twenty years, you have far greater issues than just which pony to buy.

- The Wrong Time

Are you really in a position to handle horse ownership? Can you afford thousands of dollars a month of random expenses that are far beyond your control? Do you have the hours available to care for the horse, learn the important stuff, and maintain your sanity and that of any spouses and children involved in this new lifestyle? There is no easy way out, so if you are, like many people, struggling to make ends meet, taking on a pet that will swallow your paycheck whole may not be the best choice.

- The Wrong Place

It is not impossible to keep a horse in an urban area. There are boarding stables in cities and their immediate surrounds. Even Manhattan had the Claremont Academy on Central Park until recently. But the environment isn't necessarily the best for the horse, and the expense level is likely to be astronomical. If you have to drive more than two hours to visit the horse, is that a sensible demand on your time? If you live in the suburbs or the country, do you have access to decent accommodations for your equine buddy? Are there good quality instructors within easy reach? Large-animal vets? Horse shoers? Psychiatrists? Orthopedic surgeons? If you're planning on buying a place and putting Zips Fly Bait in the backyard, do you have any clue what that entails? If the answer to any of these questions is no, then you're in the wrong place to have a horse. Rethink and find another hobby.

- The Wrong Horse

Horses are amazingly seductive. Often we horse lovers buy one based on cuteness alone. Pretty colors rank second in the Bad Basis for a Decision category. Do you know what you want to do with the horse? Do you have adequate guidance from a professional? Can you set aside your personal hang-ups, forget Flicka and The Black and all the Thelwell ponies you've smiled at from your armchair and be realistic? Do you know how to put a value on a horse? There are a thousand ways to pick the wrong horse and a million wrong horses out there. If you are the right owner and you find the right horse, you will enjoy many years of inter-species bonding. If either of you is wrong, you will have stepped firmly into Hell with both boots.

- The Wrong Advice

There are hoards of people just waiting to guide you in your quest for an equine partner. Some may even have your best interests at heart. Some my actually know something. Your best advisors will be a VET, a HORSE SHOER, a TRAINER, a FRIEND who owns horses, and possibly an EQUINE APPRAISER. If you're taking advice from the teenager next door who is a beginner taking lessons on a school horse and whose parents are in mid-divorce over the whole horse thing, you're probably looking in the wrong place for help. Hopefully this book will be a good place to start.

A BLM wild horse adoption center may not be the best starting place for a novice owner.

Chapter 1

What Was I Thinking?

The first horse that piqued my fancy was The Black, that inimitable beast around which Walter Farley built an entire stable of Black Stallion books. My weekly allowance went to the bookseller, and The Black and his boy, Alec Ramsey, came home with me. So began the horse lives of many of my Boomer cohort. It was the dark ages of the Fifties and Sixties. TV didn't offer much variety. We rode our bicycles pretty much everywhere. And we had ample spare time for reading and daydreaming.

If we were boys, we had Red Ryder six-shooters strapped to our hips, and if Roy Rogers was King, the Lone Ranger was his heir apparent. If we were girls, we had Dale Evans fringed fake-suede skirts and our own six-shooters. We all wanted to grow up to be cowboys (or Superman, but that's a different book with even more of its chapters taking place in the ER).

By the time we had reached the Age of Consent (when we could get our parents to consent to pretty much anything if we held our breath until we turned blue), most of us had tried at least once to get that Christmas pony or the birthday horse. Few succeeded. Back in the day, boarding farms were non-existent in the Northeast. I can't speak for the rest of the country, but in this neck of the 'burbs, the long driveway with the solitary and mysterious Horse Lady living at the other end was the path to Nirvana. Magical and exciting, it promised to take us places we'd barely imagined.

Thwarted in our attempts to actually move a pony and his accoutrements into the empty bay of the two-car garage, we fell on the Horse Lady like ants on a potato chip. She gave lessons on a horse old enough to vote, with lineage that invariably included a Famous Race Horse we'd never heard of. Citation must have had a lot of offspring, because dozens of his great-grandchildren came to live in New Jersey as beginner lesson horses.

When we passed the point where "buffing the saddle" with our corduroy-clad butts was a challenge, we bid the Horse Lady farewell and dragged our Parental Units to the nearest Big Riding Stable. There a man wearing a red coat and carrying a hunt horn held group lessons where we forced our friends to join our insanity and bob up and down for an hour at 0-dark-thirty on Saturday mornings until our parents simply refused to drive us anymore. Some of us were lucky enough to enter a horse show or two. Some of us brought home ribbons. Woe betided the ones who brought home the blue. We went off to college none the wiser for our experiences and were the first to succumb to horse lust the moment we located and corralled the cash cow that would pay for it.

With the next mortgage payment on hold, we stared down the dusty behemoth that bore little resemblance to the school horses our memories had embellished. We handed over a deposit check and watched the dealer's jeans recede into the sunset. Were his shoulders shaking with repressed laughter, or was it just his adopted cowpoke swagger? There we were with a new horse in hand and our dreams intact. What could possibly go wrong?

My own decision to buy a horse was, in my mind, a matter of self-preservation. Once a girl has horses in her blood, they live there forever. Living in horse country, riding other people's scary horses and spending more time butt-down in the dirt than planted in the saddle, I felt I would be safer with one, familiar, friendly critter that I could trust not to try to maim me. I was wrong. The Love is not automatic. It has to be worked at and earned. Until that first horse upended my world, the whole idea of an actual relationship with a horse was exotic, not real.

You think your horse is thrilled that you bought him? Why? Could be he was happy in his last home but his owner was less than thrilled or insolvent or died. You are not one of his herd. You never will be. You may—may—become partners, but you've got a lot to learn and hard work to do before that happens. Are you game?

Not a bad choice for a rank beginner!

Chapter 2

Drawn and Quartered

My childhood scrapbooks are filled with sketches of the horses I would own when I was grown up. It should be noted that I never once drew a barn, stable, pen, paddock, pasture, or even a large cage or cardboard box. I don't know where I though Fluffy would live when I finally brought her home, but living arrangements certainly bear consideration. My parents, wise beyond their years, tipped to this issue immediately upon learning that I'd submitted 87 entries for the "Name This Filly" contest. If I'd won the racehorse in question, I probably would have wanted her to sleep in my room. The garage would have been a distant second. I envisioned her grazing somewhere near the in-ground pool in the 50' x 80' suburban New Jersey backyard.

From the vantage point of my subsequent 48 years of experience, I now realize she'd have eaten that patch of grass in under an hour and been gone down the street shortly after. When we draw our fantasies, we don't often consider that horses eat. Then the food goes south and comes back out. That, too, has to be accounted for. They need water, lots of it, and a nice big area to pour that back out as well. We didn't even take the dog to the vet, so I'm not sure I knew they existed. Horses came with shoes. How many pairs could even a fashionable equine need?

Years passed without benefit of increased intelligence, and so I was led to my first horse.

[Enter the Scary Mare, stage right]

From the perspective of 48 years of horse life, it appears that most first horses should probably be skipped. If we could all go straight to the second horse, we'd be a lot happier overall. Dealers see first-time buyers coming. They recognize us by the checkbooks clenched in our hands and the copy of Equinomics 101 stuffed in our back pockets. Then there's the total lack of brand-name, horse-imprinted clothing. Dead giveaway.

I certainly fit the profile of the idiot newbie, and I got just what I deserved. I'd been riding for seven years followed by an enforced abstinence of another eight or so by the time I bit the bullet and gave in to my daughter's (you didn't think I was going to take responsibility for the decision, did you?) begging for a horse. She was only seven, but even she knew a loser when she saw one. She took one look at the chewed-up Appaloosa mare and burst into tears. "I wanted a horse!" she wailed. "That looks like a *cow!*" Yup, they saw me coming from miles away. The mare had been standing in a field for six years since her last foal, according to the dealer. "So she's quiet," he told me.

What did I know? Having given birth myself, I could relate to still being tired six years later. We shared a bond in the universal female experience. She and I would recuperate together. The price ($850) was reasonable. If I'd boned up on my horse trading, I'd have known it was more than reasonable. It was near killer price. I was only a step ahead of the slaughterhouse on this purchase. Pleased as punch, I patted her scruffy, tailless butt and grinned. This is my horse, I thought.

As it happened, the dealer ran a large boarding business, which took care of the first question of the day, to wit: "Where are you taking her?" Not surprisingly, they had a stall available in The Pit—the barn with the leaky roof, poor lighting, and the longest walk to anything I could possibly want to do while I was there—and I signed up without thinking twice. The whole truck-and-trailer thing had not as yet impinged on my reality, so choices were limited. I could ride her to my house a mile away and tie her to the tree in the back yard till the neighbors caught wind (literally and figuratively), or I could leave her where she was.

I dragged the "quiet" mare (who had incredibly heavy feet) and my sulky daughter to our new digs in the dark outreaches of the farm. I had a horse. The horse had a stall. Someone would feed her, I was pretty sure. Beyond that, I had no idea. I only rode horses. I'd never had to look at the business end of the business. Mine came fully groomed, tacked up, and ready to ride. This one was scruffy, naked, and already standing in a pile of manure.

"There's a tack shop over by the driveway where you came in," the dealer offered as he slithered by the open barn door. Tack? Of course! I'd kind of figured it came with the horse. I was wrong. Off we went to find all the goodies that would make this $850 horse shine like the sun and keep us safely on her back.

Little did I know that the price of the horse was only the tip of the iceberg. Years later when I worked for a dealer myself, I delighted in escorting newbie owners out to buy the necessities of horse life. Spending other people's money is much more fun than cranking up the balance on your own credit cards. But in that moment I was to learn a hard lesson.

I bought a brand-new saddle, the only one they had. It took some time to figure out it didn't fit me. The bruise on my pubic bone had to fester before I admitted I'd been led down the rosy path. Did it fit the horse? Who knows? I couldn't tell you what size girth they handed me, either. The pad was white, I do know that much. It looked like the pads under the saddles I'd been riding in for a thousand years, so it had to be right. Actually it kind of disappeared under the saddle, but no one told me that was a bad thing, so I went merrily about my shopping and added a bridle, bit and reins to the pile.

Brushes, shampoo, a bucket, sponges, and a bag of horse cookies filled the counter. My daughter eyed the rack of riding breeches and boots. Probably not a bad idea to pick up something less obtrusive than the flap-thighed twill leftovers I still had salted away from my youth. I left the shop over $2000 lighter in the wallet and not a penny smarter than when I walked in. In 1985, $2000 was four mortgage payments' worth of silly.

I owned the mare for about six months. In that time the critter patiently put up with my daily rides to "tune her up". She wasn't as patient about my daughter's riding lessons. Now that we had a horse, we eschewed the school horses and opted for the badly-fitted saddle and disappearing pad on our very own. By the time I had the mare muscled up enough to be considered fit, she'd figured out that neither my daughter nor I was adept at rodeo work. The kid hit the ground no less than twice during each lesson, and I earned my second-ever concussion. When I came to, I dragged the mare to the dealer's door and requested a trade-in.

Not surprisingly, he was more than happy to take a few hundred more dollars and the mare in exchange for a truly handsome gelding. Prince was not without his problems, but he did a fine job for three years before something bad happened to his feet. He went on to cart handicapped children around for a bit while I moved on to other horses.

An important sidebar here is that that witchy mare who greeted us every day with her nose in the corner, her rear end threatening, and her ears laid back in a "Not YOU again!" expression of displeasure eventually made another family very happy. With no demands made on her, no ill-fitting saddle or hour-long lessons, she lived a good life as a babysitter to the children of an experienced horseman. She wasn't a bad horse. She was a bad horse for me.

Sometimes the least likely horse makes the best partner…most often, not.

Chapter 3

The Good, Bad, and Worst of Choices

Still in all, I hadn't fared as badly as some first-time buyers. I often think about the pretty young woman at a barn where I worked who had somehow wound up with an unbroke colt. For months we watched as she fussed over him and worked up to the daunting task of saddle-breaking. If she'd asked for help, it wouldn't have done much good as none of us had any experience in that area. It was obvious, though, that her plan to sit on him while he was cross-tied in the barn aisle was not the best we'd ever heard. Day after day she dragged a stool near him and gradually added more of her weight as she sprawled across his back. He, eyes bugged and ears laid back, straining at the cross-ties, suggested she might want to reconsider her desire to ride him at all. We, terrified at what looked like an accident that could take out several of us along with her and her horse, suggested she might want to move her act to the round pen.

"Round pen" wasn't a verb yet back then. We didn't "round pen" horses. There just happened to be a pen on the premises, and the pen was circular. By the light of a gorgeous sunset, she pulled an overturned bucket up to the horse while I held the lead. She never actually got on him. As soon as he felt her foot in the stirrup, he walked away, causing the bucket to fall over. The racket sent him bucking and her flying against the pen rails.

Eventually she recovered from the broken pelvis. The rest of us never did.

Then there was the guy we all called "Daryl" (from a Bob Newhart comedy sketch involving none-too-bright brothers) who bought a cute horse that was in on consignment. I was just a tad concerned when Daryl introduced himself as a trainer from "out West". I'd have had more confidence if he'd been able to pick up the horse's feet. Or identify them. It was one of his hoof-picking efforts that landed the horse on his side in the wash stall hung up by his halter. Still, selling horses was part of what paid the bills for that barn owner, and Daryl's money was as good as anyone else's.

The horse would have been a real find for an experienced horseman. He was a green-broke baby with nice conformation and a decent attitude, and he probably went on to have a good life somewhere as someone else's second or third horse. But he and Daryl hit the road together despite the obvious disconnect. Occasionally the fellow would work up the nerve to ride the horse down the hill to the woods, but he'd generally eat dirt and come back up leading him. That went on for weeks.

The end of Daryl's horse life was marked by two more events in quick sequence. First, he had finished his horse stuff for the day after the usual dumpage and leading-home exercise, and he had led his horse out to the pasture for turnout. He was in the company of a hoot of a guy, a beginner rider who had bought a wild-eyed former barrel horse that would have killed a lesser man, but this guy had all the guts in the world from years of motorcycle mania. The biker unclipped his mare's lead and swatted her across the butt with his cowboy hat to send her off. Daryl, sensing machismo in the air, turned his baby loose and gave a swat with the new black cowboy hat he'd taken to sporting.

The young horse, however, wasn't thrilled. Instead of taking the cue to make a quick exit, he kicked hard, breaking Daryl's hand.

But three's really the charm. When Daryl finally recovered enough to revisit the scene of his idiocy, he discovered the horse was now terrified of him, his hoof pick, and his hat. That was the icing on the cake for our young wannabee cowpoke. He went home never to return. Later he called and asked that the horse be put back up for sale. A far wiser move than I would have expected.

That sale/boarding/lesson barn afforded ample first-horse opportunities for our educational benefit without putting us in direct danger. They included a city boy, an actor by trade, who bought a darling gelding, another in the parade of bad first-horse pairings. In his case, the horse was fine. He had come in on consignment from someone who had used him as a child's western pleasure show horse. He had the moves and the attitude and was cute as a box of puppies. We all rode him the day he arrived and fell in love with him. I even took him out on a long trail ride to check his attitude, which was exemplary.

But no horse is the right horse for a non-rider. If you haven't learned which way to face in the saddle, you've got no business owning a horse. In this case it was the horse who suffered. His new owner had more guts than common sense. We'd been warned not to let him take the horse out on the trail alone. We were to call the barn manager if we had any inkling that a solo ride was afoot. But eventually he managed to slip away unnoticed. When he came back, the horse seemed a little gimpy, but it was some time before we got the whole story. Seems the guy got a little ahead of himself and let the horse lope along the road where fresh oil on the loose gravel sent him sprawling. The owner said later that he thought the horse's scream was a bit disproportionate to the size of the accident, so he just hopped back on and rode him home.

The horse continued to limp for a while, and no amount of cajoling could convince this owner to call the vet. He avoided the barn and didn't respond to phone messages. Eventually the barn owner took matters into her own hand and called for help. The horse's broken leg had already healed badly by then, and he was lame for life. The owner stopped coming to the barn entirely and stopped paying board as well. Like Daryl, he asked that the horse be put back on the block, but by then the animal was permanently lame, not just from the accident, but from shoes that had grown nearly into his feet while the barn owner tried to get permission to have the shoer out to take care of him. I left there before I found out what happened to that little guy.

[Welcome the $400 Internet Special Mare]

For some time my daughter was into training horses here at the farm for other people. One such horse should have been the poster horse for inappropriate matches. The owner, a teenaged girl, had found the horse online and bought her without seeing her in person. The horse was a very cute, if oddly-conformed, baby less than two years of age, the result of a backyard breeding effort. The owner was a rank beginner. Two years later, the owner had a broken collarbone to show for her silliness, and the horse, at four, had never been tied or led successfully. She hadn't been thoroughly groomed in years. She suffered from a skin disease and the leery attitude that derived from having been followed around the pasture by her owner who swiped at her with a brush whenever she stopped moving.

A word on "backyard breeding" is appropriate here. For those readers unfamiliar with the concept, there has long been a belief held dear by horse owners that if you buy a mare and she doesn't work out (or you need extra cash or an income source for some sort of tax abatement for your "farm"),

"You can always breed her". Most mares who wind up belonging to folks who subscribe to this notion are not top-quality in terms of conformation or attitude—traits passed on easily to offspring—and would not ever, ever be considered breeding stock by any serious horse breeder. Even if the owner throws caution and cash to the wind and purchases "cooled semen" from a top stallion and a visit from the AI Guy (that's the vet who's adept at artificially inseminating mares with said product), the good genes from the high-end absentee daddy rarely completely overwhelm the questionable ones contributed by the cranky, four-legged-lame, cross-eyed, parrot-mouthed momma. The result adheres to the odds. Though the occasional winner pops up, most offspring of such liaisons are middle-to-low in quality and soundness.

The filly in question was at the low end of the scale. Once here, she proved to be a fairly adept learner but with more bad habits than a spoiled child. Months of work ensued, and eventually the filly was rideable and would stand tied and behave appropriately. There was a suspicion of a neurological problem, which was confirmed in a mandatory vet visit, but the owner was pleased with the horse in spite of that. The shake-down cruise, when the owner got to ride the horse and put her through the paces she'd paid for her to learn, went swimmingly. All was well when we delivered the filly to her new boarding home.

All continued to go well for a couple of weeks. The owner wasn't specific. She just mentioned in an email that there had been an injury. It is possible that the neurological problem that made the filly a little unsteady on her feet in some situations might have contributed. It's even more likely that the owner's lack of experience, which had not improved during the training period, was to blame.

Had the teen actually done the necessary legwork and found a horse that was appropriate to her skill level and her needs and kept her in a setting where she had the support of experienced horsemen, things might have ended differently. Whatever injury the horse and rider suffered might never have happened had the filly belonged to an experienced owner. But there's no accounting for (or stopping, apparently) Love at First Google.

[Welcome the Non-Horsy Parents' Choice Award Winner]

The girl, young and newly ensconced in a riding lesson program, loved horses. She was progressing at a pace which led her ignorant parents to believe was startling. Before her first year on horseback was over, Mommy Dearest decided little Tonya would have a horse of her own to cherish and grow with. Sadly, Mommy hadn't read a book like this one, so she didn't know that there are evildoers and forces of good within the horse world, and she was misled into buying a horse that might have been a fine second or third horse, but wasn't a good first-horse match for her daughter.

Naturally, Tonya was thrilled…for a day or two. But it quickly became apparent that riding one's own horse all alone without benefit of trainer is not the same as riding an experienced lesson horse (the saints of the equestrian world) under the direct management of a knowledgeable professional who oversees every yank and kick. Before long, the mare's head-tossing, arm-yanking habit irritated and frightened the child, and those awful words, "I hate this horse!" rang out.

Logic would suggest that this might be the moment when parents would step in and sell said horse with a promise of something better to come with a few more years in the lesson program. Logic doesn't have to listen to a small child shriek. I've been there. As much as my daughter disliked her stubborn and ill-mannered mare, the thought of selling her tweaked every inch of her heart into a rapture of depression and torment. Getting her to turn the mare loose required major manipulation and the purchase of a more suitable horse, and even then the tears continued for months and the recriminations for years.

Tonya's mommy opted for a different approach, and one that I do not condemn but certainly don't recommend. She decided to learn to ride so she, herself, could bring the mare under control.

If there's anything about that which seems sane, you need to find a new hobby, because riding isn't healthy for you. Here we have a non-riding mother who believes that in a few lessons she will master horsemanship to the point of being able to retrain a horse that strikes fear into her heart and her daughter's. It takes years to learn enough to be completely safe on a good, well-mannered horse. To think that a few lessons will do the trick is insane!

I learned about this situation from a fellow boarder at the farm where the mare is being kept. She wanted my advice so she could help the mother fix the horse's problems. And there we have the second brick in the wall between the owner and any hope of saving this situation. If the only advisor she can find has to resort to emailing a friend for second-hand advice, she's in bigger trouble than she knows.

I demurred, of course, since giving advice on a dangerous situation sight-unseen is like a diagnosing a disease over the phone. No one wants to be the bottom line when there's a good chance someone is going to be injured or even killed if the advice is misinterpreted or simply wrong. Liability has long arms and a voracious appetite. My suggestion was that my friend tell the mother to sell the horse and wait before buying another one, or, failing that, find a really good trainer and move horse and child within easy reach for the duration. I'm waiting to hear the outcome, which I hope will be better than some of the other stories I've related here.

If there's a moral to this chapter, it's that green riders shouldn't own horses. Leasing works. Taking lessons is good. But if you've just got to have that Horse Owner title on your resume, at least take a knowledgeable trainer or rider along with you when you shop. Sometimes a pair of eyes un-misted by horse lust can be invaluable. Your life and the horse's may depend on momentary clarity and presence of mind, so don't take that first-horse purchase lightly.

Sometimes your best horse is one that belongs to someone else and comes with an instructor. Lessons are always a good choice.

Chapter 4

Too Hot, Too Cold, and Just Too Smart

The three bears had nothing on us horse owners. If we manage to avoid the First-Horse Mismatch scenario, there's plenty of opportunity for goofs and slip-ups yet to follow. Take basic first aid, for instance. How much do you really know about the inner workings of that massive creature nibbling at your shoelaces? Believe it or not, horses are not cats or dogs. They have parts that don't exist in either of those species.

For example, horses can't vomit. It's a hobby well-loved by dogs and cats, but it's totally unavailable to your horse. If he eats something he shouldn't (like the plastic bag with the horse cookies and the paper money and coins someone left near the crossties), it's not coming back in the expected way. As a result, it behooves the owner to be aware at all times of what is within reach of the horse. Not all horses are omnivores. Some draw the line at old socks, others at the expensive feed you just bought. My daughter's grade gelding enjoyed the occasional fried chicken lunch if it was within his reach. My Paint mare is partial to mocha cappuccino. Only the Morgan and the Appy mare had truly exotic tastes. It was the mare who scarfed the above-mentioned cash. The Morgan preferred creosote paint straight out of the can.

So if you've already passed muster as a first-time owner in the sense that both you and the horse have survived the initial days of your relationship, you may still have much to learn.

[Enter Morgan Gelding, stage left]

By the time Rat joined our growing string, we'd been into horse ownership for several years. I'd been working part-time at a barn to offset board, and ample mistakes had been made and survived. We'd learned, for instance, that it's crucial to take off those winter blankets occasionally as you never know what you'll find underneath. We found ribs and hip bones sticking out.

Negotiating with a recalcitrant barn manager is a talent few owners master. It's important to remember:

You have the right to complain, and you have the right to leave, but you don't have the right to get even.

Every boarding farm has its own style. If you don't like where your horse is living, move him. That sometimes turns into a very emotional decision and a hard experience, but it's your best option. For many horse owners, the barn staff and other boarders become a family even closer than the blood relatives who think the whole horse thing is ludicrous. Divorce is hard enough when only two people are involved. Leaving a barn family means removing people, horses, and all the other stuff that goes with both and relocating all of it somewhere else in a great black hole of unknown dimensions: A New Barn. Anticipation of the trauma is usually worse than its reality, but avoiding it often keeps horse owners plastered to the walls of a place that is totally unsuitable.

When we had to make the move (not the first and certainly not the last), Rat was a two-year-old just learning to pull a cart. The other two horses in our little herd were well-settled, and it didn't take long for them to put back the weight they'd lost. Rat, however, was a challenge from the start, which requires another caveat. If Grandpa decides Granddaughter needs a horse, don't leave them alone together. That's how twelve-year-old girls wind up with yearlings to raise and train. If Gramps shows up at a horse show, make him turn over his wallet and checkbook to you before he gets out of the car, or you'll be hauling home a horse you didn't know you'd bought and that no one is capable of handling.

So the Morgan came to live with us just before we moved to a new barn. To say he was an interesting horse is akin to calling Mad Max "quirky". Still, he'd been a fairly easy horse to start even for an inexperienced child and her insipid mother, so what could go wrong?

The creosote thing we'd learned about early on, so we knew to keep open cans of anything away from him. What we had not learned was that it wasn't really a lack of good taste that drove him; it was boredom and a highly intelligent mind.

The first time we got a call from a barn owner that we needed to "get over here right now! You won't believe what Rat is doing…" we were a little startled. Fortune smiled on us. His first adventure involved finding a western saddle and blanket on the railing of the indoor arena where the horses at that barn were turned out for brief periods while their stalls were mucked. The finding wasn't the adventure. The burying of the pad in the footing was. So was his new-found ability to remove a Blevins buckle and bury the resultant loose stirrup. He was working on the second stirrup when we got the call.

Not long after that he unearthed a whip left in the dust by the trainer. He used it to drive the rest of his turn-out buddies around the arena till they were in a lather. He was a horse with a sense of humor and a great smile. He was not a horse to be ignored or taken lightly. He was also not a horse for just any boarding farm.

When you find yourself with an equine smarter than you are, it becomes imperative that you inspect the prospective digs in detail and quiz the barn manager until she's ready to hand back your security deposit. One manager thought it was hilarious that Rat would spend all day working his way into the middle of a coil of barbed wire left in the pasture, then work his way back out and start again. We didn't see the humor in it. Many days of scouring the pasture unearthed more wire and lots of other intriguing (from a horse's perspective) goodies. The barn owner loved us as we busied ourselves clearing the wreckage and repairing fences and stall walls. But that didn't prevent Rat from finding the hole we'd missed in a remote corner of the pasture fence. We met him on the road. We were driving to the barn to ride. He was off on a ramble around the neighborhood. We learned to carry a lead rope in the truck until we could find another boarding farm.

Even the highly experienced, professional horsewoman who was dealing successfully with the controlled chaos of twenty-six horses on about eight acres wasn't quick enough to notice the little black horse taking the bolts out of the shed row gutter until said gutter hit the turf. We never knew where he slept at night only that it wasn't in the pasture or in his stall. He always got home for breakfast.

Horses like that one are priceless, not just because they tend to train easily and be excellent companions, but because they are a learning experience of the type psychologists call "flooding". They throw so much at you at once and so quickly that you either learn or die. In one respect, this is the ideal second or third horse. Just when you think you know what you're doing, just when you're starting to harbor Professional Horseman fantasies, a horse like Rat comes along and shows you your folly.

Lest you think Rat was one-of-a-kind, another horseman with, coincidentally, another Morgan, told me that her horse delighted in stealing tools from her father's back pocket as he worked around the barn. The *piéce de resistance,* however, was when Daddy was working on the barn roof and Horsie, smiling that special Morgan smile, moved the ladder.

I don't want to be accused of being a "breed-ist", so I'll only add one more Morgan episode. At the barn where Rat spent his days playing in barbed wire there lived a Morgan cross named Sonny. Sonny was the wise-guy who discovered that standing in the manure pile between two barns, he could stick his head into the barnyard and cadge treats from whoever happened to be handy. Since standing in manure is not the best thing for horses' feet, and as we boarders were engaged in a major renovation of the property anyway, we decided to cut off his access to the pile. Fence posts had already been put in place, but the project had been abandoned. A few miles of plastic clothesline strung between the posts made a passable fence that was safe enough and tight enough for the circumstances.

Watching Sonny drop to his knees and limbo under the bottom line was enough to render even me speechless. Where there's a willful horse, there's a way.

The takeaway message here is: If you want to know what's wrong with your farm, turn a smart horse loose on it for a day. Better yet, get someone who's already been abused and trained by a really smart horse to drop by and point out all the errors you've made. You may have to go pick him up at the Home where he's been living since he finally sold that intellectual equine, but it'll be worth the effort.

Lest you misunderstand, let me assure you that a smart horse may be "just right". "Too hot" is another category entirely. The "Too Hot Horse" can be the baby that pops out of the bred mare you bought at the urging of a horse friend who needs for some unfathomable reason to see you in pain. It's not possible to have your horse friends checked by a psychiatrist. Most are too crazy to agree to that. So you'll have to learn to read motives on your own. Obviously that was not my strong point.

Pokey, a poor, underweight and foundered Paint/Thoroughbred cross mare off the Paint Horse track, might have been my "Too Hot Horse". She still might be if aging and a list of physical ailments wasn't taking the spring out of her buck. The warm, cozy feeling of caring for a pregnant mare is seductive. The mental image of that tiny replica squishing unceremoniously out of your mare's hind end brings many horse lovers to tears. Baby animals of any species are almost unbearably cute, and they offer the opportunity to test out our best, highest selves. We get to start from scratch with a creature who has not felt dirt beneath his feet. We adore the whole experience.

In many ways, I was very lucky. Pokey, lunatic that she might have been (and, at this writing, still is), was an excellent mother. That meant I didn't have to learn all the fun parts of raising a foal on my own. It meant that the bangs and bruises I got during the process of figuring out how to make Zip into a riding horse had plenty of time to heal between episodes. I never faced the challenge of bottle-feeding or convincing an imprinted foal that he is not human. I only had to do the usual breaking and training, and the most painful and hazardous of that was absorbed by the Sacrificial Daughter.

By the way, if you're going to raise young horses, then plan ahead and have a child first. A ten-year-old girl is just the right size to pop on an unknown equine of rideable age, and whereas you'll most likely splat, she'll probably bounce, and her ER and recuperation time won't impair the family cash flow to the same grievous extent.

Among "Too Hot" horses, we can number many thoroughbred race horses adopted from the track. With good retraining and patient handling, they are amazing animals to own. Racehorses are trained from birth to be handled and worked around. They learn to ride in trailers, to get up before dawn, and to do whatever is demanded of them. They are generally bred to be fast. A fast mare and a fast stallion will generally produce a fast baby. He may not be fast enough for the track, but he'll likely be faster than you, as a first-time owner, can imagine.

[Enter Paint Mare, Snorting]

The allure of the homeless horse is strong. I was no longer a beginner by any stretch when it caught me. I wanted to help a horse and a friend, and I had choices. There was the pinto Morgan mare with the badly scarred leg, the gelding with the questionable past, and the mare off the Paint horse track that was foundered, skinny, and pregnant. The chance to get two horses for the price of one—and cheap, at that—and indulge my baby-raising fantasy at the same time was too good to pass up.

Pokey turned out to be a fine horse, though her feet and her allergies (we'll talk about relocating horses to different areas of the country later) left her retired at the young age of eleven. We had a great time while it lasted. But I will never forget that moment when I took her .37 speed index (meaning she was only a third as fast as the fastest horse in her last five races) the wrong way and put her up against my daughter on her Morgan gelding. That was the first and last time I ever asked that horse for speed. Even several years of barrel racing didn't prepare me for what happens when a racehorse opens the throttle.

The retired racehorse straight off the track is a project for an experienced trainer and until the retraining is complete, a beginner should probably think twice about taking on a horse bred to run. It's such decisions that interventions were designed to prevent. Racehorses are trained backwards. When a beginner rider panics, his instinctive reaction is to regress into an ape-like hunker over the front of the saddle and pull hard on the reins to suggest to the horse that stopping is an option. A racehorse is trained to run faster under those circumstances.

That said, however, many rescue groups take horses from the track, give them serious professional retraining, and re-home them successfully with novice riders. It's the "professional retraining" part that's important in that sentence.

But racehorses aren't the only adoptees available. For a while, when the hormone drug Premarin was popular for Baby Boomer women in menopause, the foals dropped by the mares who had to be kept pregnant all the time in order to produce the main ingredient, pregnant mare's urine, were appearing at auction and at rescues by the tens of thousands. Some 60,000 per year were available at one point. Now that other options are available and most of the production facilities in Canada have closed, they are a shrinking part of the vast adoptable horse market.

There is nothing wrong with adopting a Premarin foal provided that you are experienced enough or wealthy enough to train the animal yourself or hire a professional. Any foal, regardless of genesis, is a guaranteed two years of feeding, vetting, and housing without any payback in terms of riding or driving. A horse isn't ready to be broke to saddle or harness before the age of two, and even then many are still not physically (or emotionally) developed enough. Breed matters in this case, but two years is the minimum. If you can afford to keep a foal then also pay for someone to do the training when the time comes, you can wind up with an amazing horse. I would never discourage anyone who wants to help out a horse in need, but if you can afford all of that care and training, you can also probably afford to buy a horse that suits your needs immediately. Keep that in mind.

The same theory applies when you think about taking, as I did, a bred mare. It holds up as well when you decide you just have to attend the herd reduction ("dispersal") sale at the local breeding farm. Or when you hear through the grapevine that the Paint or Appaloosa horse breeder in the next county is selling uncolored babies (not white, just lacking the markings characteristic of the breed) for $50 to $500 a head.

Two years is a very long time, and there are no guarantees that you will have a good horse in the end. There are crazy horses just like there are crazy humans. Genetics accounts for a lot of things. With the new information available from animal behavior researchers like Temple Grandin, it's possible to shave the odds in your own favor, but still there is always a risk. I often tell buyers that a horse is not an investment. Spend $100 to adopt a horse off the track and he may turn out to be a great buddy or illness or quirkiness may render him a total pasture puff just days after he joins the herd. Spend $100,000 on a dressage horse, and he may make the Olympics or go permanently lame a week later. Horses are living beings. They fall down. They get hurt. They get sick. They get stupid. If you want to invest money, find an investment that can't eat toxic hay and die a nasty death.

A foal gives you the opportunity for many more years of forking over big bucks to care for a sick animal if you've chosen poorly or your luck has simply run out. Little Brittany isn't going to stand by while you send her pony Fluffbudget down the road because he's never going to be rideable. If you are not strong enough to fight the good fight when your child (or your spouse) can't say good-bye, you do not need to risk taking on 30 or more possible years of bondage.

Of course many first-time buyers get the picture about Bringing Home Baby, and they proudly stand firm in the face of cute foals. But those same tough souls fall apart at a BLM (Bureau of Land Management) wild horse auction. At a recent sale, I watched two completely different scenes unfold within a few feet of each other.

On one side of the pen was a gentleman who had just bought two mustangs and was being helped by the BLM staffers to load them onto his trailer. He had brought one stock trailer with no divider. There was a big question about whether or not two mustangs unfamiliar to one another would ride cheek-by-jowl without freaking out. The buyer was inexperienced, never having owned a wild horse before and giddily (hysterically) proclaimed such to anyone within earshot. The staffers were excellent and managed to drive the horses through the chute and into the trailer without bloodshed. The buyer's voice was shrill with excitement and terror as he bid everyone farewell and started down the driveway, the trailer rocking with the motion of two horses trying to get away from each other in close quarters.

On the other side of the pen was a woman who had many years' experience with BLM mustangs. She'd paid for her adoptee the previous day and was now spending her second day in the pen with the mare, gently working the animal to get her familiar with the halter and the leading process, and starting the bonding that would have to happen for any successful training to take place. It was a lovely dance to watch. By the end of the second day, that trainer was able to quietly lead her new mustang out of the pen and onto the trailer, and there was no doubt that, barring the unforeseen, they would have a long and happy relationship.

Many trainers will tell you that there are special methods that work with wild horses and many current trends in training that don't. If you're not sure that you know what to do, and you don't have professional backup, you should avoid this situation and find a horse that is already broke, trained, and ready to be your friend.

This brings up the current status of horses in this country. In 2009, as I write this, the financial situation worldwide is disastrous. Trickle-down economics is in full swing, and the horse market has crashed with horrible effect. In some areas of the country, horses are being abandoned in their pastures. Others are being turned loose in rural or residential areas to seek out food and water on their own. Still others are being sent to auction and, unsold, left tied to the fence at the auction house, unwanted and homeless.

Many of these are horses that should probably have been euthanized by their owners. Sick, injured, lame, or very old horses are expensive to care for, and in a near-depression economy, are at the bottom of the priority list. Some rescues are now offering low-cost euthanasia for owners of such animals.

But there are also family horses, show horses, school horses, and training-aged horses with tremendous potential finding themselves homeless because their owners have decided, wisely, to put feeding their families ahead of feeding their pets. Many of these animals are advertised online at such places as Equine.com, Dreamhorse.com, Lancasterhorse.com, and Craigslist. If you have a friend or a paid professional who can accompany you (owners do lie, though we'd like to pretend they don't) while you do hands-on visits, you may find the perfect horse out there just waiting for a nice beginner to take him home.

A caveat is needed here. If you are looking at free or low-cost horses because you can't afford anything else, you should not be horse shopping. Period. If I didn't make this clear before, let me repeat that the price of the horse is the least of the expenses you will face over the years. A regular poster on a horse forum recently berated me for suggesting that if the buyer needed to make payments over time on a reasonably-priced horse (in this case, the price was under $2000), she couldn't afford the animal and should not be enabled in her quest to become a Horse Owner. In too many cases, that's how horses came to be on the "Free to Good Home" or "Please take my horse by the weekend or he's going to auction" list.

But if you have the wherewithal to help a horse who otherwise might suffer, then by all means let the shopping begin!

Under no circumstances should the beginner buyer buy a horse online without seeing him in person, preferably more than once. Even better, he should visit in the company of a sane adult horseperson. Even a video is no substitute for watching the horse being ridden and riding him yourself. If you aren't able to ride, you probably shouldn't be buying. Take lessons, then shop. And I say you need to visit more than once because a horse may have a bad (or an exceptionally good) day. You want to be sure there are no 1) drugs, 2) underhanded methods, or 3) frizzy brain hairs involved.

I did mention in the title of this chapter the "Too Cold" option. In the horse world there are three kinds of horses apart from but directly related to their breeding. There are "hot" horses (thoroughbred racehorses, Arabian horses, and some other light-boned breeds tend to fit this group), "warm" horses (Warmbloods of various varieties, crosses between thoroughbreds and Quarter Horses or draft breeds), and "cold" horses (many Quarter Horses, most draft breeds, and crosses between the two).

A "hot" horse will tend toward quickness and speed, may be highly intelligent, and will generally be difficult for an inexperienced rider to handle. If the ad says "intermediate" or "advanced", or the scale in the ad suggests the horse has a hotness level of 3 or higher on a 1 to 5 scale, he is in no way suitable for a beginner. Picture handing the keys to your new Ferrari to your neighbor's 16-year-old son. I rest my case.

If you see "WB" in the ad, that's a specific designation. "Dutch Warmbloods" are a breed, not just horses from the Netherlands with a particular hotness level. Mid-hotness horses can be excellent for beginners as long as the discipline the rider has chosen allows for a certain amount of flair and speed and big movement. Hot and warm-blooded horses are generally not acceptable for quiet, calm work in the Western Pleasure show ring.

The third category sounds as if it might be a mistake on my part, but I'm here to tell you that it is quite possible to buy a horse that is too mellow for your taste, even for a beginner. A horse bred and trained for Western Pleasure is often from a genetic line that is difficult to fluster but may also be difficult to get moving if you are of a mind to pick up the pace or change your style. The beautiful Appaloosa gelding I bought for my significant other to ride is just such a horse.

Though he serves well as a horse for a beginner with some experience and some guidance, under a non-rider, Dakota is a non-mover. I'd chosen him in part to use for beginner lessons for friends who prefer the solid, secure feel of a chunk of a horse and a big, heavy saddle with a handle. Big D is just such a horse. Unfortunately, he demands that his rider give him constant direction and be confident about it. The humor in the Marine sergeant kicking and flailing and flapping his arms while Dakota stood placidly in the middle of the riding ring waiting for me to give him instructions was not lost on anyone but the rider. Particularly poignant was the fact that the Marine's diminutive girlfriend who weighs less than the saddle and was also a non-rider, was able to move the big horse through serpentines and segued within her first hour to fancy leg-yields at the walk. Love at first sight in either direction is not to be second-guessed.

So, yes, there is such a thing as a too-cold horse. If you are a beginner, and you are not taking lessons, you should avoid a horse that has a hidden start button. You will view him as stubborn and difficult, not safe and sane, and your relationship will deteriorate very quickly.

Chapter 5

The Sensitive Spirit

Most often, the Sensitive Spirit is a rescued horse, but that's not always the case. It stands to reason that a horse that has been abused, neglected, misunderstood, or simply forced into a career not of his choosing will become sensitized to human interactions. If Fuzzbutt came to you in a trailer barely worthy of the name or was the animal you just had to take home when you found him tied to the gate at the auction house long after the sale was over, odds are he has some issues.

The trick is not to get so caught up in the Flicka Syndrome that you lose sight of your own capabilities. If this is a first horse, you're insane to take one that may have killed his former owner. If you're naïve or inexperienced enough to believe what the seller told you about the horse's history, you need to be accompanied by a responsible adult on future buying trips. We are at a point in the horse business where many perfectly good horses are homeless. But along with the good ones are the ones that only a professional should consider taking home, and then only if his insurance is paid up.

There are crazy horses. Insanity is not restricted to Humankind. My favorite crazy horse story was told to me by the man himself. His erstwhile girlfriend had covered up an illicit romantic liaison by bringing home a few horses from a "buying trip" out West. In the end, my friend's take on it was that she'd done her dallying, then in an effort to cover her tracks, stopped at the first place with horses in the pasture and made an offer on whatever was there. The group included a horse which, had he been human, would probably have been diagnosed as psychotic with homicidal tendencies.

My friend described the scene. The horse was impossible to handle. In the field, he ran himself headlong into the barn wall repeatedly. He had attacked my friend and anyone else who tried to get near him. Obviously not a suitable riding horse, he had a very brief stay at my friend's farm before he was sold.

My friend was at work when the buyer arrived to pick up the horse. His work phone rang, and he answered to find his very upset girlfriend on the line. The buyer had brought extra hands to round up the recalcitrant equine, and they'd managed to corner the animal and shoo him into the trailer. But minutes later, as the trailer began its homeward trip, the horse lost his mind and kicked his way out. The girlfriend wanted to know what to do.

Guilt-ridden over the damage, my friend told her to pay the buyer for the damage to the trailer and let him out of the deal. She hung up. Shortly, she was back on the line, even more hysterical than before. The buyer, she said, had told her he didn't need to be reimbursed; he'd still take the horse, but that to get the horse on the now flattened trailer, he would need to give him a shot. She told him that was fine, at which the buyer retrieved a shotgun from his truck, shot the animal, dragged him onto the trailer, and left. Sounds cruel, I know, but some horses are simply "sideways", as the old-timers say. Missing a few brain hairs. Not too tightly wrapped. Damaged goods. Crazy.

If you're reading this with a tear in your eye for the horse and an emotional commitment to help the next homeless beast you encounter, you need, in my opinion, to take up a different sport. Horses, like people, need to be assessed with a calculating eye. A horse that is born with problems isn't going to get better just for you because you own everything ever written by Buck Brannaman. He may make a fine pasture pet if you're in the market for a very expensive lawn ornament. He may never, never make a riding horse.

On the other hand, you might have encountered a horse like the one another of my friends currently owns. She bought him for all the wrong reasons. His history was sketchy, but most of it was perfectly solid. She believed she was buying a horse in far worse condition than he proved to be. In her case, the horse was actually fine. He'd been spoiled by his last owner, a teen-aged girl. Rumor (the horse world thrives on rumor and innuendo) had it that the horse had been abused. He did have a scar on the top of his head that could possibly, just possibly, mean a "war bonnet" had been applied to set his head. A "war bonnet" is a cable head-setting device that relies on pressure and, in the wrong hands, pain to cause a horse to drop his head for western pleasure or hunt-seat exhibition. But at some prior point the animal had been a noteworthy show horse, bringing home ribbons over fences on a regular basis. Mistreated? Perhaps. Spoiled? Definitely. Abused? Maybe. Sensitive? Oh my, yes! And very, very smart.

As it happens, she was exactly the right owner for the horse. With superhuman patience, she spent months working with him until he was putty in her hands and a joy under saddle … at two gaits. At last count she was still working on getting him to stop bucking at the canter, but she was on her way.

But my friend is not a beginner. A novice, she'd worked with horses, owned horses, and loved horses long before this sensitive soul crossed her path. A beginner would have been over-horsed by this fellow, frightened by his threats, and generally unable to do more than drop cash by the carload while she spent her horse time watching from the safe side of the fence while her equine "buddy" lounged in the pasture. This woman was able to apply reason to her obsession and produce a nicely recovered animal.

She is the exception. This is a "don't try this at home" scenario. Which brings me to another point: if you find yourself with a Sensitive Spirit and without the experience and patience to work through the problems, make sure you are not alone on an isolated backyard farm. Surround yourself with experienced horse people and bond with them.

This seems a fine moment to interject that many horse shoppers look for horses that compliment their own craziness. The rider who has been scared to death by a serious accident may opt for a horse far quieter or less energetic than her needs actually require. The temptation, particularly now when so many animals are being subjected to abuse and neglect, to credit every equine misbehavior to human failing is also ripe.

It can feel romantic and terribly *au courant* to take in a sad case. But often it's fear of having to deal with a perfectly functional horse with all the accompanying equine foibles that causes a buyer to take home an animal that will never be anything but a quirky pet. How easy it can be to chalk up your inability to improve your skills or overcome your terrors to the poor animal's need to be "brought back gently"! No riding, no threat. Sometimes that's exactly what the doctor ordered for both horse and human. I suggest only that you be fully aware of your motives before you choose your new best friend.

"Green Horse, Green Rider"

Chapter 6

You're Never Too Young... Or Too Old

But your horse most definitely can be. I've already discussed the fatal errors that can accompany the purchase of a foal by a first-time horse owner. I won't belabor that except to scream, *don't do it!* But babies fresh out of the mare aren't the only too-young youngster you need to be wary of.

Remember the story about the teen who bought the yearling filly on the internet? There was more wrong with that decision than just a beginner horse person launching a project for which she was ill-equipped. There's also the issue of problems that can arise later if the buyer isn't experienced in assessing very young horses.

The day the Morgan, Rat, came into the boarding barn where I was boarding and working he cast a spell over all of us. His registered name wasn't "Rat", it was Willowrock Ultimately, an "own son" (that is, not a great, great, grandson of a nephew) of UVM stallion Ultimate Command. Sounds amazing, doesn't it? We had no idea what it meant, but all of us sighed and nodded knowingly about how impressed we were, hoping, I think, that someone who actually knew something might happen by and clarify what we were supposed to be impressed about. That never really happened. The barn owner did manage to steal a photo of the sire so we could all see what this baby might look like when he was grown, and that was about all the information we had. That, and that Rat had been taken to the annual state breed show and made Weanling of the Year, and he was nominated (meaning he placed high enough, and his owner-breeder paid the fee) for the following year.

If you've never seen a baby Morgan of the classic, "type-y" style, they're just too cute for words. Baby Rat stood just tall enough to reach the tip of his nose over the bottom half of the Dutch door of his stall, so our first impression of him was pointy nose, long whiskers, and the breed's signature bugged eyes. Hence the nickname. The barn owner said, "He looks like a giant rat!" So much for class.

I didn't intend to own this horse. Buying Rat was a result of a Grandparent Intervention gone awry. My daughter was in love, and I was leery. Her grandfather had offered repeatedly to buy her yet another horse, hence my earlier warning about frisking grandparents for checkbooks and cash prior to allowing them contact with your children. I'd paved the way out of the possibility by calling ahead and warning Grandpa that Jess was far too young to break and train anything bigger than a hamster. A plan congealed, which I thought was a shoo-in. Jess and Grandpa and I would meet on his turf for lunch; she would plead her twelve-year-old heart out to make her case, and Grandpa would lovingly demur, urging caution and doling out hugs and some other gift as a consolation prize for good decision-making.

That's why you never leave kids alone with grandparents. We weren't at the restaurant more than a salad's worth of minutes when Jess pleaded and Grandpa buckled. I was floored! I scrambled and came up with the plan that Jess could work with the youngster for two pre-purchase weeks under constant supervision. If she and the horse emerged unscathed, we'd revisit the question. I figured that would buy me enough time to find a better way of circumventing Grandpa's Checkbook. We all shook hands on the deal (my father was not at all impressed by my bone-breaking grip and nose-to-nose stance), and went to work on the project.

As it turned out, Jess was more than okay at handling the baby before we bought him, and later she would once again be more than okay. It's the middle piece, where Grandpa wrote the check and the baby's training had to begin in earnest, that bears inspection.

Rat had a natural inclination to learn. That was helpful, but certainly nothing we could have surmised from our first inspection of the colt (and he was, by the way, a stud colt, not a soft, squishy, girly little gelding). The pre-purchase vet exam turned up nothing more exciting or deterring than a mild club foot that never did cause the horse any problems. We knew there were training issues. The swollen purple hoof prints on the chest of the barn owner's husband suggested that bathing was not one of Rat's favorite things. And he could only be groomed from his left side. And he loved his hair to be braided, but only from the left side. And he hated fly spray on either side. We wondered aloud how his breeder had managed to get him show-worthy, but we knew she had, so we persevered.

He was a "long" yearling—meaning just over a year old—when he moved into our herd. By the time he was a yearling-and-a-half, he had already begun to explain to us that he needed to be kept busy at all times. This "Too-Smart" horse could find more ways to occupy himself than a room full of toddlers, and none of them was acceptable. It's not standard for a horse that young to do any work, but we had to find something, and quickly. I barely had money for board. Repairs to the barn were not in my budget.

So there came a day when a fellow boarder suggested that we might want to borrow her cart and harness and teach Rat to drive. Did we know how? Uh...

Rat turned out to be better at it than any of us was. When no one noticed the missing girth on the "saddle" of the harness, and the weight of the sacrificial test-driver (the crazy man who bought the rank barrel horse, remember him?) flipped the cart on its back, Rat took it all in stride. The shafts whipping upward past his head didn't faze him, nor did our efforts to tie the harness together with a western girth and baling twine. So adept was the horse, that a month later we were proud owners of our own cart and harness and a driving horse we could take on the road without concern. Sweet!

But the training process was not without pitfalls. Too young to be ridden, longeing (working on a long line with a trainer on the ground) was our only hope for teaching him. He did fine until we screwed up. This is where a pro would have known exactly what to do. We, on the other hand, just sat around and yelled at each other and cried a lot.

Our screw-up came in the form of a badly orchestrated effort at ground driving. That's when a trainer—not us—attaches two long lines to the horse's bridle or halter and runs them through a contraption strapped around the horse's girth line. This surcingle is supposed to keep the lines from tangling and maintain them at an appropriate height for the work being done. We were so clueless, I'm surprised we didn't just tie the whole thing together with baling twine. But we had the borrowed equipment, and so we gave it a shot. In minutes Rat was stuck in the corner of the square "round pen" we were using and panicked. No one was injured. No one was even seriously upset. But Rat decided from that time forward and forever more that working in a circle with ropes tied to him was not going to be in the cards. He lived 16 years without changing his mind. Any effort to correct the problem resulted in the "trainer" having the "trainee" firmly planted on top of her, his eyes rolled back into his head and his body shaking like a pride of lions had just entered the arena.

None of that had to happen. Watch someone really professional work a horse from the ground. There are ample tapes and video clips available. Watch *The Road to the Horse*. Watch *Dancing With Horses*. Watch anything other than a rank beginner wreaking havoc on a young, impressionable horse's mind, and you'll have more information than we had.

Because we lucked out and just happened into a really, really good horse, this green horse/green trainer situation turned out fine. Few people are that lucky. Figure the odds and decide if it's worth the risk. Getting rid of a really good, well-trained horse is hard enough in the current environment. Getting rid of one that needs retraining or has to have his owner sing "It's a Long Road to Tipperary" before he'll let her tighten the girth is much harder. Getting rid of the one who put his back feet through the barn wall while his anxious owner was showing us how nicely he stood for grooming is nearly impossible. Those are the ones that wind up at auction or "free to good home including all tack and one small child" on Craigslist.

I'll assume you've got a firm grip on the "too young" concept. But what about "too old"? Conventional wisdom has always been that the ideal first horse for a newbie is an older animal, done with all the hysteria and shenanigans, and ready to just cruise along babysitting his partially-competent rider. Seriously, it's every mother's dream to find such a critter for her horse-smitten child. Or for herself. The vision of a slightly grizzled equine head clutched firmly by an awe-struck human graces the pages of books and magazines daily. It's that warm-fuzzy thing that makes even non-horse folks think a horse would make a nice pet.

And it's a wonderful concept. But (ah, there's always a "but"), there are a few caveats I must share. They are equally serious though not as life-threatening as some of the other misfit issues.

You know you're looking at an older horse when 1) the seller can't seem to find the papers, 2) the horse is listed as "safe" or "retired schoolmaster", or 3) the horse has more gray hair than you do. Older horses are never listed as "prospects". Older horses have done all their prospecting and are simply living out their days hoping for the best. Older horses can and do rate high on the "hotness" scale, but it's a different scale. A hot geriatric horse may blow up, but it won't last long. He may buck and fuss, but he's more likely to just glare and grumble. You can talk to an older horse, and he'll ignore you and keep doing what he was doing before you entered his space.

Older horses are generally kinder and saner than they were when they were younger, but they are also set in their ways. Sure, you can teach an old horse new tricks!

[Enter: Leo, the Geriatric Dressage Beast, stage left]

When I bought Leo from his last owner, the plan was to make him a school horse. He was already older than the rest of the herd, and despite some indications that he was capable of diabolical machinations, he seemed sane enough. He needed some retraining, was just a tad spoiled, and had an internal clock that was more accurate than my digital watch when it came to meal times and precisely 45 minutes into a lesson. He could turn on a dime and smash his young student rider into the gate before she could scream, *"Whooooa!"*

He'd had ample experience, though I was unsure of the discipline. He seemed like a western horse who preferred to go under English tack. Or vice-versa. It was a little hard to figure out his preferences. What was immediately apparent was that tacking him up always resulted in a threat on his part to bite his human and a threat on my part to practice my kick-boxing lessons.

In time all of that changed, and it took far less time to get Leo to give up his stubborn ways than it did to train Rat. So on the learning curve, Leo was much faster with a longer payoff period for the amount of effort invested.

In time he went from English school horse to sometime barrel horse to dressage horse, and he thrived on lessons in any discipline I chose. The more we worked, the more amenable he became. It's been years since the last time I sported a bruise on my shin in the shape of the steel arena gate. And he loved going out on the trail as long as it didn't involved walking down the road alone. Woods, fine. Road, not so much. Whatever. We do it, just not happily.

But Leo was only about 15 when I bought him. Not young by any means, but also not yet encumbered by health issues that tend to afflict aging horses. Now, eight or so years later, he's got arthritis, some almost as old as he is, throughout his back leg joints. He still works fine as long as he gets his supplements. Those aren't cheap, but they're certainly cheaper than joint injections, and don't require vet calls. But I've been lucky. Not only is his condition readily controllable for a reasonable sum, but there's nothing else wrong with him.

Any horse older than about four is likely to have some physcial issues. It comes with the territory of carrying some bouncing chunky monkey for endless miles over interesting terrain. A horse that has been a "good horse" may have been used far more and sport far more damage than the horse no one wants to ride because he's got a few too many frizzy brain hairs. So be forewarned: find the perfect older horse, and he's likely to break down before you pay off that new saddle you bought him.

In addition, recent research has shown that horses really evolved to be about 15 hands high. In ads, height shows up as a number followed by "h" (hands) or "hh" (hands high). A hand is four inches, so fifteen hands is 60 inches (five feet) at the highest point of the withers. Some people consider a fifteen-hand horse to be too small. Anything much smaller may be pooh-poohed as a pony, though the standards for those are way smaller than fifteen hands.

The current fashion is Bigger is Better. When you saw WB in the listing and discovered it meant "warmblood", you might also have noticed that the number following it was over fifteen. Warmbloods often range in the 16 to 18-hand-high area. That's tall. That's very tall. It's too tall for an older rider who is not tall.

At 5'4" and not young, I'm fine with a 15hh horse. My 16hh Zip is fine as long as I have a tree handy to climb to get back on him should I come off. There's no mounting from the ground in my future. If anything, my mounting blocks are getting taller so I can basically ascend the stairs and step easily onto his back.

This lead to an interesting interlude just a week ago when I decided he was back in shape enough for an outing along the road and into the woods. I'd latched the gates, so I had to dismount to lead him through. When I got to the driveway, I climbed up on my two-step mounting block and stared up at the stirrup which seemed to be hanging at eye level. I tried repeatedly to get my leg to bridge the distance, but it just wasn't happening. I chalked it up to too-tight pants, but too-old legs are more to the point. So back we went to the ring where my three-step block awaited, leaving a trail of open gates behind us. I remounted and rode him back out through the gates wondering what would happen if I had to get off.

I did. He was so excited to be out and about on the new spring lawn grass that I had to fight to keep him from eating while we rode. That's an absolute no-no. Opting for training over fighting, I dismounted and lead him the rest of the way along my planned trail and back to the barn. I could have enjoyed his contrition and remounted, but there was nothing tall enough other than the fence (I stopped launching myself onto his back from the fence some time ago when I got a case of sanity for Christmas) to stand on. It was hot. I was sweaty. I vowed again not to own a tall horse unless and until I'm reincarnated as a supermodel with legs up to my shoulders.

But, I digress. The subject was aged horses, not aging riders. Not all older horses are hale and healthy, and frequent vet calls can sap your disposable income faster than a house full of teenaged boys on a pizza bender. When my daughter got married a few years ago, we decided that her oldest equine buddy, twenty-six-year-old Grady, would stay behind for me to care for until his demise, which, as it turned out, was imminent. She hadn't even gotten all of her stuff out of my house before he developed a tooth-root tumor. Of course we didn't know that was what it was. The vet didn't know. It was a rare condition that even the equine dentist had never encountered.

Between July and November, when he was finally euthanized, Grady was hand-fed three times a day, feed soaked and commercial chopped forage fed in lieu of the hay he could no longer chew. His teeth began to fall out. There were vet visits three times a week, punch biopsies and blood drawn. Samples went out to places like Cornell University Veterinary School. In all, more than $2000 in vet bills crossed my checkbook during that time period, and that doesn't count the cost of all the exotic feed or the time required to see to his care.

When it was finally agreed that he was not going to survive, the visit to the vet clinic to confirm that with the ultrasounds and x-rays and poking and prodding that ensued cost another $1700. Jess, beside herself with grief, wanted the remains cremated so she could keep them. That's $850. And Cornell wanted the head for research. Shipping was another $200.

Granted, even a young horse can rack up vet bills, but the odds begin to worsen as he gets older. If you can't bear to part with a horse till he meets a natural end, you could be looking at bills that will curl your eyelashes. Can you afford it? The odds improve with a horse in the 8 to 15 age bracket. Keep that in mind. And keep in mind that even experienced horse owners haven't always seen every ailment to come down the horse pike. Your ignorance can cost you and your older horse more than you would imagine.

Chapter 7

Who Ya' Gonna Call?

Considering all the possible ways the wrong horse may attach itself to you, there is an additional bit of information you will want to keep in mind. That is this: The value of the horse is the price someone will pay for it.

In other words, another way you can wind up with the wrong horse is by buying into someone else's estimate of the value of the horse and overpaying as a result. Even though at this writing the horse market is depressed, there are plenty of very expensive horses available. Like the folks who choose their wines based on price instead of quality, horse buyers have a tendency to believe their own hype. If Trainer X tells you that you need a horse in the $50,000 range in order to succeed in your chosen sport, and you like Trainer X, you will find yourself drawn to horses with that sort of new-luxury-car price tag. Whether or not the horse has earned that price is open to discussion.

Keep in mind as we enter the realm of the Bad Advice Horse that this designation is by no means the fault of the horse. Horses have no intrinsic value. They are very cool animals who would much prefer to be lounging about green pastures with their buds than dealing with humans in any way. But we humans have a need to label and categorize and rank and denominate everything. So we put a price on horses in order to facilitate their transfer from crazy horseperson to crazy horseperson.

As a certified appraiser, it both tickles and pains me to even write this chapter. In a perfect world, horses would be free to be used by whoever needed them. Their care and upkeep would be the responsibility of their current human companions, and when they needed to move on, they would do so. They would leave my herd and move next door to yours just because it's nicer there or because you need a horse that likes to jump, and I have one that I'm not using.

Were that the case, I'd be out of a job, which would not be a bad thing in my opinion. Writing appraisals for estates and court cases and insurance loss cases is hardly pleasant. But everyone, including our dear Uncle Sammy has to have a finger in the pie. Which reminds me that you mustn't forget that any horse you buy that outlives you is going to be inherited by someone you specify and taxes will have to be paid on his value. Isn't that a hoot? Even that half-lame rescue pony has a value that the government wants to be sure to duly note and account for.

It serves all horsemen well to be realistic in the dollar values they place on their equine partners. Realism isn't often part of the horse world, so it's a stretch to expect that the seller you're dealing with is going to be totally up-front and honest. Even if she is, there's that sphere-of-reality disconnect that makes communication such a fun sport. She says her "dead quiet" trail horse is worth $4,000. You look at Flinger dancing on the end of the lead line and think maybe she's talking about a different horse. Your trainer hops aboard and pronounces Flinger a bit flinchy but trainable at, maybe, $3000 plus six months of her training and boarding fees. Your budget says $1500 tops for horse, tack, and a barn to keep it all in. Can't we all just get along?

The way an appraiser figures out the "real" value of the horse is to do some comparison shopping. He finds two or three other horses in the same area of the country that are doing the same job, are roughly the same age, same breed, same conformation, same training level, same health status, and does the math. Adding points for good stuff (six months with a Big Name Trainer, parents who lived to be 30 and never had a sick call, a nice attitude), and deducting points for bad stuff (that weepy eye, the part of the seller's jacket that's between the horse's teeth, the sketchy identification), and averaging it all out, he comes up with what your horse should probably bring on the open market. Nothing is carved in stone, no matter what the seller says.

You can do the same thing at home if you take the time and know how to turn on a computer. You can go to websites like Equine.com, Dreamhorse. com, Agdirect.com and others and plug into the search the exact horse you're considering buying and the stipulation that the search include sold horses. Assuming you are at all motivated, it will take you a few days to determine whether the asking price is in any way reasonable for that horse.

When you do your search:

1. Make sure the horses you compare are in your neck of the woods. Why? Because a western trail horse is less valuable in an area with no trails. A jumper is less valuable on a working ranch. A ranch horse has less value where there are no ranches.

2. Choose the exact same riding discipline you intend to pursue. You may be okay with taking a horse that excels at dressage but is slightly lame and using him on the trail, but for comparison purposes, you need to make sure the parameters are as close to identical as possible.

3. If you're a beginner rider, you need a beginner horse. Make sure you are looking at beginner horses in your comparison. Words like "family horse", "husband horse", and "school horse" all mean "beginner". Words like "foxhunter prospect" do not.

4. If you know the breed of the horse you're considering, make sure you choose other horses of the same breed. In some areas of the country, certain breeds are more popular than others, so there will be more of them, but the prices will likely be higher. Don't compare an Appaloosa with a Quarter Horse on the East Coast, for instance. Quarter Horses are ten times more popular, so the Appy will be priced lower. Don't even consider using exotic breeds in your comparison unless the horse you're considering is of that breed. It doesn't matter what a beginner horse of the Akal Teke breed sells for in your neighborhood. Odds are it won't be the same as what a Pinto pony sells for.

5. Look at the pictures and videos and, if at all possible, at the horses themselves in person. Cute horses tend to be more expensive (though not better in any particular way) than ugly horses. This especially holds true with kids' horses. Kids love cute horses, and moms and dads love kids. They'll pay more to see their kid on a cuter horse. Better photo ops. Sellers know this, and so do appraisers. Be the Appraiser. Add dollars for cuteness. Cuteness means that the animal gives a pleasant overall impression from its refined little head to its flowing mane and tail and monogrammed, designer blanket.

6. If you're shopping for a well-trained horse, avoid comparisons with "prospects". The word "prospect" in the horse biz means the horse may do well at a particular activity because he has the right build, an appropriate attitude, his parents did well at the sport, or he

has been tried a few times but not actually trained to do it. You can't compare futures at this point. You can only compare actual experience.

7. Don't include in your market comparison horses that are being sold because the owner is financially distressed. The market part of the appraisal requires that you match the situations as closely as possible. Horses being traded on the open market in a fair trade deal will be priced considerably higher than horses that are on their way to auction because the owner can't pay the feed bill. Don't expect your seller to be thrilled when you tell her that you want that $4000 horse for $200 because you saw a similar rescue horse for that price. That's just silly and a bad negotiating tactic. Go adopt the $200 horse and stop trying to do the comparison.

8. Sometimes horses seem to be priced far too high. Odds are you're just not getting some important point about their training or history. If a horse seems too far out of the average range that you've been noting, it probably has won a lot of ribbons or produced a lot of babies that have. Don't count those horses at all. Sellers often inflate their opinions of their horses on this basis, but the price estimate is not grounded in reality.

9. If you're shopping via the internet or newspaper ads, don't compare those horses with prices of horses that were sold at auction or in a dispersal sale at a breeder's farm. That's not the same market, and it doesn't compare.

10. If you're not sure, hire a trainer or an appraiser to do the work for you.

You probably noticed that there are markets where horses are a lot cheaper than what you're looking at. If you think you can handle it, a livestock auction is cheaper than a want-ad horse. It's like buying at a garage sale instead of going to Macy's for that purse. A dispersal sale or other "forced liquidation" (meaning they had no choice but to get rid of the animals for whatever reason) invariably means lower prices. But you have to know what you're looking at to shop at those venues. If you are a beginner, odds are you can't just eyeball a horse standing in a pit at an auction and make a good judgment as to its character and ability.

Here is where things can get a little tricky. You've figured out you need professional advice, but you have no clue how to find a professional. Again, the horse business has its shady side, and you are likely to be headed into the shadows if you don't start on the right foot.

I'm going to assume that you have heeded at least some of the warnings I've already issued and are taking lessons, leasing a horse, or otherwise already involved in the horse world prior to setting out on a buying spree. The barn owner or trainer at the barn where you've been spending your time may or may not be the best person to guide you, but they can guide you to someone who is. There is no certification required to own a boarding farm, and trainers are generally uncertified as well, though there is a process available. I've known barn owners who were charged with the care of horses but knew less about the animals than they did about nuclear physics. Liking the animals and having the money and guts to rent or buy a barn and set up a business are all that's necessary. And anyone who likes the term can call himself or herself a trainer. But in the end they will both have to associate with actual equine professionals, to wit, the vet, the horseshoer, possibly a certified equine dentist, and a local feed store. Get the names and numbers of those professionals, and you've got a start on guidance that might help rather than harm you. You're going to need them all anyway, so put together a Black Book and use it.

Start with the horseshoer. Find out when he's going to be visiting and make an effort to be there when he is. Engage him in conversation. In some cases this may be your most difficult moment, as shoers are notoriously funny and not a little quirky. It comes from standing upside down under horses for many years. Still, make the effort. Ask if he's come across any horses for sale. Ask who in the area is a reputable seller and who you need to avoid. With luck, you'll be in for an uproarious time filled with tales of wonder about Horse People He Has Known. Take notes if you have to to keep the names straight.

The vet or his office manager is invaluable since he's going to have to check the horse over before you settle the deal with the seller. Don't think for a minute that you should skip this important meeting. Once you've been through the mill enough to be able to judge a horse without help and if you can afford to maintain one that has health issues, then you can cheat and go without a Pre-purchase Exam.

Most vets are fairly adept at dentistry, so you will not necessarily need the dentist at this point. You will, however, want to call one if there's any question about the condition of the animal's teeth or his age, and especially if your vet doesn't really like to do dentistry. Many don't. It's not cost-effective for them, so they don't get as much experience as the dentists who do nothing else.

The feed store staff, if they like you, will fill you in on such subjects as which farm is chronically behind on feed bills or buys bedding only when they have a bunch of horses to sell. They will be most useful after you've made the decision to buy and need a place to keep the horse, or when you aren't sure whether or not to trust the seller. You'll need to be a little cagey as reputable staff won't simply blurt out the information for fear of losing customers. But you'll be surprised at how quickly they'll rat out the ones they don't care about losing. Those are the same ones you won't care about dealing with.

"What are you looking at?"

Chapter 8

The Pre-purchase Exam

One last word before we move on to the post-trauma portion of the book.

To recap, in spite of all I've already said, you're going to buy a horse. You may not be sure why, and this might turn out to be the biggest decision in your life made entirely on a whim, but you've got your heart set on bringing home something equine. You've got a list of seventeen horses from equine.com and dreamhorse.com that are good possibilities, and you're in the process of narrowing it down to the few that you will actually meet in person and consider seriously as additions to your family.

My personal vet, Dr. Christopher Fazio, VMD, was kind enough to take time from poking and prodding Zips Attitude in search of a new reason for the most recent bucking spree to talk to me about what a new horse owner should know regarding the possibly fateful, often-ignored pre-purchase exam (aka "vet-check"). I asked Dr. Fazio for his take on the necessity of the exam, what parts are most vital and useful, and for any words of wisdom he might have for first-time (or even third-time) horse buyers.

"The most important for them to remember is, especially if they've worked with a professional in the loop, whatever your plans are at home, include [your chosen professionals] in your decisions. Everyone could go get a horse, build a place, build a paddock, build a pasture, but in all honesty the important thing is don't forget about the person that got you into this." That person might be the experienced boarding farm owner you've made friends with, the instructor from whom you've been taking lessons on a school horse, a trainer under whom you've been studying, or perhaps another type of horse professional. The point isn't which one to pick, it's to pick as many brains as you can, and try to stick to the ones that have experience and your best interests at heart.

That said, think carefully about how much you can safely afford to spend, and how much you can realistically afford to lose. It's that latter number that will really make the difference when you are committing to buying a pet that will cost, at minimum (based on estimates from the American Horse Council and the American Association of Equine Practitioners) five dollars per day to maintain ($1825/year). That's without board, veterinary expenses, shoeing, or equipment.

I suggested to Dr. Fazio that most older horses—the most rational choice for a first-time owner, particularly a beginner rider—won't pass a standard vet check. It's a given that an older horse will show evidence of arthritic changes in his joints, particularly the hocks and often the pasterns. He may also have the beginnings of a cataract or two or be a little wheezy. Knowing that, is it worthwhile for a buyer to even bother with a pre-purchase exam on an older horse, particularly since older horses are frequently less expensive than younger ones?

The answer was an equivocal yes. "I think in this day and age the price of the horse does not necessarily dictate [the necessity of the exam]. A less expensive horse to one person, to them may be a big chunk of change out of their pocket. I think those are as warranted to have a pre-purchase done as a $20,000 horse." What Dr. Fazio does, however, is offer a scaled-back version of the exam at a lower price—enough information to be reasonably sure that the horse will be "serviceably sound" (healthy enough for the work the owner intends to do with him), but without the more expensive x-rays and blood tests that might be more important for a performance horse, a show jumper, or an eventer.

A full pre-purchase exam consists of the vet checking the horse externally for signs of injury, then checking his heart and lungs for obvious problems. A lameness check will include visual examination of the horse both standing still and in motion at various gaits with and without a rider. Hoof testers will be used to check for internal hoof problems that might not yet be causing obvious lameness. Teeth and eyes will be examined and assessed, and major joints—fetlocks, knees, hocks—x-rayed for signs of damage. If the horse is a high-end registered show animal, blood testing may be necessary to prove parentage or to avoid some of the hereditable diseases such as HYPP that are common in some blood-lines. The scaled-down version will eliminate the x-rays and blood tests unless there are clinical signs of lameness or pain or you simply have extra cash to invest in this venture.

Naturally, the younger the horse, the more vital the buyer might find the pre-purchase exam. I confess that I've only had two done over the years, and the first was on a yearling. A yearling with health issues may have as much as thirty years of problems ahead for you to deal with and expenses to divert your cash flow and will be virtually impossible to resell for that reason. An older horse—say, twelve or more, which is considered "aged"—may have a few minor flaws but still be sound enough for enough years to warrant the purchase price and the eventually-increased necessity for vet care. It is absolutely vital that you be merciless in determining what you can really afford.

Finally, Dr. Fazio brought up an important point. If you're buying a horse for a child, don't tell the child until after the pre-purchase exam. Little Stacy won't care that Dontouchme is lame as a three-legged chair or suffering from terminal flatulence if he's got pretty eyes and the seller put a bow on his tail. "A thousand-dollar horse can easily become a $20,000 horse if there are problems", and Stacy isn't going to be able to cover that out of her allowance.

One caveat: A horse is a living thing. A pre-purchase exam does not guarantee continued good health, just health status at the time of the exam. Don't blame the vet if six months down the road Fuzzbutt breaks a leg or develops an illness. And the vet's estimate of the horse's age is only approximate. If the seller is lying through the Fuzzbutt's teeth, a vet check isn't necessarily going to call him out on the lies. But it is definitely a good place to start.

Chapter 9

Myths Busted So Far

1. Anyone can and should own a horse.

2. Horse ownership is the key to happiness.

3. All horses are created equal.

4. Everyone in the horse business is trustworthy, loyal, helpful, courteous, and kind.

5. There is no "unwanted horse problem".

6. Small children are capable of making life decisions for their families.

7. If you buy a mare you're making a good investment because you can always breed her if the riding thing doesn't work out.

8. The price of the horse is the biggest consideration.

9. Beginner riders can grow and learn with a young horse.

10. All horsemen are good with horses.

It's hard to imagine that there can be more caveats ahead, but there are. You now know that your suburban neighborhood will probably not be home to the Great Horse of your dreams, and that odds are you really can't afford a horse now or in the immediate future. You know that anyone who tells you horse ownership is easy is lying. It should be clear that there is an amazing amount of learning involved in everything to do with horses, and that it's a very steep learning curve. By the time you start to feel confident and see some real returns from your learning process, you'll be too old to remember what you were thinking when you bought the horse.

Let's leave the small stuff behind and move into something most novice horse owners don't think about: LIABILITY.

Chapter 10

A Word About Horse Owners and the People Who Sue Them

There are several levels at which we can enter the discussion of the liability a horse brings to the table. At the very lowest, simplest level, we have the basic liability of owning something with a brain and a body big enough to win in a tussle with a small car. When you buy a horse, you also buy the responsibility for everything that horse does while in your employ.

Some years ago I received a photo in the mail. It was a nice shot of the tree in my front field, a gorgeous landmark oak, but the picture still came as a surprise. As it turned out, photography was the chosen rehabilitation activity of a friend of a friend. The photographer was rehabbing from a collision with a horse that had gotten loose on a local highway. She hit the horse at the standard speed of 50 mph, according to reports. The horse just stepped in front of the car, and boom! The equine died. The driver wound up spending considerable time in the hospital with permanent brain damage her take-home gift from that horse encounter.

If you think something like that is a rarity, think again. In rural areas like this one, livestock loose on the road are nearly as regular a sight as road-kill deer and other critters. Since cows and horses tend to be bigger than deer and raccoons, they are less likely to be hit unless the driver is distracted or drunk, but they do get smashed up with fair regularity. The liability for the accident rests solely with the horse owner or caretaker, depending on the type of horse-keeping that's going on.

Even if your facility is completely secure (and I seriously doubt anyone can call anything "completely secure" when a horse wants to conduct the testing himself), there's a little something called the "attractive nuisance". Horses rank up there with unfenced swimming pools. If you've got a neighbor dumb enough to feed her infant to your horse, even if she's trespassing on your land

and holding the child in the air in front of the equine as some sort of offering, it's your liability. She can't be held accountable for stupidity. You are the one maintaining the "attractive nuisance" that is your equine buddy. People with and without common sense are attracted to horses, hence the "attractive" part. That horses will bite, kick, and otherwise maul said people constitutes the "nuisance" piece. Together the concept suggests that unless you can wall your equines out of sight of the public and far enough away from humankind to keep everyone safe, you are in trouble from the get-go. If you throw your horses out into the small paddock you so lovingly fenced with wood and wire just inches from your neighbor's property line, you might as well just hand over your house, car and other valuables now, because eventually someone will come to take them from you.

And if your state has an "Equine Activities Liability Act" that keeps bad riders from suing their instructors when they face-plant in a lesson, don't assume you're covered for everything. Generally the laws stipulate that the victim must have been participating in an equine activity. Spectators, student's parents and siblings, neighbors enjoying a confab with your nasty mare are not subject to the strictures such Acts represent. They can sue you for every bump and bruise (and the emotional stress that comes with being assaulted by your best buddy, and they may win.

Take it a different direction and consider the damage a loose animal can do to property while he's rambling around the neighborhood. Even if the bush he eats kills him, you are responsible for replacing the bush and paying whatever "pain and suffering" award the court might deem fit to the bereft owner of the late shrub. Someone I knew had what could have been a comical moment when the cow he was transporting untied in a horse trailer made her escape in the middle of town. She probably knew she was headed to auction and wanted to plead her case to the general public, but regardless of motive, the result was property damage. As locals and police tried to corner her, she did some visiting, remodeling a porch railing and doing some gardening along the way. The owner was mostly relieved that the creature had been caught and he'd finished his trip without further incident. Then he received the bill for the damage and the fine from the town for his cow's illegal rampage. Believe me; what he paid was far more than the cow brought at market.

In a horse-oriented neighborhood, folks tend not to be as quick to sue since the next horse to escape might just be theirs, but as development encroaches on open land, more and more often horse farms are hemmed in by big houses with fancy landscaping and "Keep Off the Grass" signs. Those people do not see the humor in hoof prints on the bocce court. Every blade of grass your horse eats, every pile of manure he leaves along the roadside, every snack of neighbor baby is your responsibility.

Insurance helps. If you own your own farm, you have to have it anyway, and high-dollar liability policies are actually quite reasonable in price. I recently upgraded from $500,000 to $1 million for about fifty dollars added onto my existing policy. I may amp that up again if I start having more visitors or more urban types move into the neighborhood. For now, considering how little I do with my horses in terms of transport or lessons and how lazy they've proved themselves to be when it comes to planning a getaway or staging an attack, that's sufficient. If you don't own a farm, you still need insurance, so add that to the price of the horse, which, you might have noted, is growing faster than the crabgrass you haven't had time to address since you've been so busy horse-shopping.

If you show your horses or drag them somewhere to ride on trails, insurance is even more important, not just the liability kind, but the health and life policy on your horse in case disaster strikes and next year's mortgage payments seem destined to live at the vet clinic where your buddy is recuperating from a run-in with a squirrel or a bite of a nice yew tree.

And that's still not the end!

If you have expensive tack, that may be covered for theft and destruction under you homeowner's policy, but you'll need to check on that and possibly specify and pay extra for big-ticket items. If you board at an establishment with other people (pretty common, since horses generally don't live alone), there's always the chance that someone will take exception to something you've done and set you up for a lawsuit that you never saw coming.

[Enter, the Evil Horse Person]

This can be a fellow boarder who just doesn't like your attitude or the barn owner or manager who is behind on the rent and needs some extra money.

An acquaintance related a story that bears repeating. Her parents had bought her several show horses from a local dealer and boarded them at the dealer's place. The dealer was of the manager/trainer variety who tend to set up programs of showing and training that can suck in the unwary non-horsy adult who is bedazzled by the glitz and in love with the shiny-eyed joy their horsy child is exhibiting. It's a type of cult that is insidious and common to all sports involving children, so don't think you're immune if you manage to sway little Crystal from her horse fetish with dreams of Olympic Gymnastic Gold.

As time and the show season wore on, many miles were covered and much money was spent on travel and expensive clothing for children and horses alike. All went well until a particularly pricey item turned up missing, left behind, it would appear, at a show venue where chaos had overwhelmed common sense and sharing of items came into play. Tears and recriminations ensued, but nothing prepared the parents of this young rider for the law suit filed by the barn manager who suggested the item had been stolen by them for gain. Bad feelings all around ended with an exodus from the barn and everyone lawyering up.

Not what you envisioned when you googled "horses for sale"? Sadly, it's not an uncommon tale. I don't have fingers and toes enough to count the lawsuits to which I've been privy, sometimes from both sides. "She touched my stuff!" isn't reserved for badly-behaved tweens on summer vacation. My own "stuff" was compromised by a fellow boarder, so I know the drill all too well.

In my case, the offending boarder was unhappy with some news I'd delivered, so she took her anguish out on my young daughter's stuff. We all degraded ourselves into whiny nastiness before the problem was resolved with another exodus. No lawsuit, but the bad blood spread widely, pooling around us as we moved from barn to barn with the offender hot on our trail. Some people just can't let go. Horse people, who are generally obsessive anyway, can't let anything go.

If, in your newfound wisdom, you take a horse on trial to your barn for a period of time (a common practice, though not always the best plan), and that horse becomes ill, injured, or otherwise incapacitated, you're done. You will probably owe the full purchase price to the seller. At very least, you'll be liable for vet bills and recompense for whatever losses the seller will take on a future sale of the animal. On the flip side, if said beast injures a horse on your property or where you are boarding, and the injury can't be chalked up to lack of sense on the part of whoever is doing horse management there, that also is your deal, vet bills, replacement cost of the injured horse, and whatever else someone can think of to sap your savings included.

Let me be the first to tell you that your options for suing the seller who sold you the horse that threw you into the ER five minutes into your first ride are limited. There is something called "Due Diligence", which means that you, the buyer, did your research. It might also mean the seller did his research if he bought the horse for resale. You both have a responsibility to make sure you know whether this is, indeed, a horse, and to the best of your ability have scoped out any issues that might turn up to cause the deal to be less than ideal and admitted same to each other. Unless the horse was stolen, unless you can prove that the horse was drugged when you bought it, unless you have ample evidence in the form of veterinarian's testimony, unless you have a lot of money, you are not likely to win. So let this caveat stick in your mind: You bought it; it's yours.

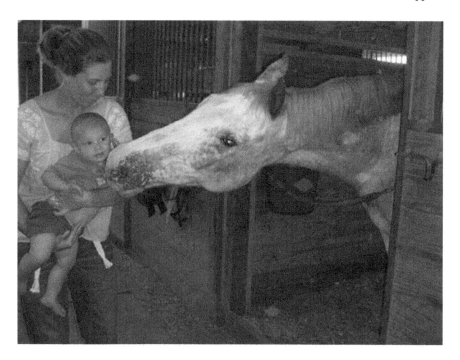

A budding horse-whisperer: "Tell your mom you'll stop stuffing corn up
your nose if she buys me."

Chapter 11

Attention, Shoppers…

I'm assuming that you are about to ignore everything I've said so far. You probably would have thrown this book away by now if you hadn't already made up your mind to buy a horse whether you need one or not and were hoping for guidance. So a word about the shopping process must be tossed in here.

As I type this (and probably for years after these pages have yellowed) the horse market is in a slump. That's bad for owners who have horses that they can't afford to keep and would like to sell. It's great for buyers. Talk about a "buyer's market"…! If you hang around the feed store long enough, someone will slip in, put a lead rope in your hand, and slip out again, and you'll be the proud owner of a "free" horse. It doesn't get any better for prospective owners even if they're advanced and looking for a high-dollar show horse for fun and profit.

That makes your situation as a beginner all the riskier. Animal acquisition regardless of species has a huge emotional component. All expenditures are emotional, but when the object of your desire can look you in the eye and suck your brain out, the danger of bad decisions becomes immense. I've already touched on the wisdom of taking someone knowledgeable along to keep you duct-taped to the truck while the horses are paraded by. But some of you will insist on going it alone.

There are some deal-breakers that you need to cast in concrete in your Rules to Shop By. You will not buy him if:

- The horse bites you or his owner while you are looking at him.

- Less than four of the horse's legs are functional.

- The seller can't remember where the horse came from.

- The horse attempts to kick something or someone.

- There is a hint of disease in the horse's demeanor or he is coughing loudly and dripping noxious fluids from various orifices.

- Everyone who was present when the horse was led in has either disappeared or is laughing loudly.

Those are things you can see without the help of an expert. You should have looked at pictures of some normal, healthy horses before you started your adventure. Know a swayback when you see one. Know that grey hair all over is called "roan", but grey hair just on the face and other isolated areas is called "grey hair" and indicates advanced age. Know that all four feet should be roughly alike in size and shape. Know that knees should face forward in the front and backwards in the back. Any variations in those basics should tip you off that this may not be the horse for you.

In addition, you should be prepared to ride the horses you're looking at. Naturally, you will bring along someone who is experienced in whatever discipline you intend to pursue. Bringing a western trail rider to look at an English jumper is hardly effective or efficient. But after the expert has ridden the horse, you should also climb aboard. Big hint: If you're too afraid to get on the horse now, you will be too afraid to ride him at home! Gut instinct is valuable. If it unnerves you that the seller has three friends casually holding ropes binding parts of the horse's mobility structures or his mouth is tied shut so he can't bite, you do not need to ride this horse and buying him is out of the question.

But if the horse seems kind enough to tolerate you, make sure that you ride him the way you intend to ride him later. If you are a western rider, bring your western saddle or make sure there's one available for you to use. Same for English.

[Enter, the interesting Appaloosa gelding]

I can't even chalk up my own interesting choices to Beginner Syndrome. I'd been shopping for months for a replacement trail horse that would ride western and English and maybe be suitable for beginner lessons. I had ample experience riding and buying horses. I'd tried at least six and already found two that I liked. One was vetoed by my significant other who would ostensibly be his main rider ("ostensibly" because whenever a non-horse-person type family member decides he needs a horse and asks you to find one for him, you can almost bet the farm that that person's butt will never see the back of the animal you've chosen). That horse had a "bald" (white) face and blue eyes, which my partner found distressing for some reason. The other was a nice Quarter Horse I'd fully intended to buy before the seller simply faded into the woodwork. That happens sometimes.

So when I came across the Appy at a nice boarding farm not far from home, I saw him through a haze of frustration. He was handsome. He was owned by a small child. He had no history of craziness according to the barn owner. What more could a buyer ask? He looked healthy, and as I watched the barn owner ride him first, he moved nicely. There was a little shying issue at one end of the ring, but I worked him through that in seconds. I already knew why the horse was for sale and that he hadn't been ridden more than a handful of times in the preceding eighteen months (which is what happens when you buy a horse for your kid and she changes disciplines as fast as she changes hairstyles).

I put the horse on hold for the weekend and drove my partner, Cliff, by the farm to look at him from a distance. He agreed that this looked like a good horse. He didn't feel the need to ride him.

And a nice horse he was (and still is). Dakota (why are all western horses named "Dakota"?) was easy-going and comfortable to ride. Though he was a little stubborn, he gave up any argument quickly when challenged. The seller insisted on delivering him herself rather than letting me pick him up because she wanted her daughter, his nominal owner, to see where he'd be living and approve the barn before she accepted the check. This is the best of all possible approaches for the buyer and for the seller of a family horse in which there's an emotional investment. Dakota came off the trailer without a backward glance and was as quiet on my land as he had been at the boarding farm. Score another point for the horse.

The interesting part came when I actually started riding him regularly. See, I'd done some western riding and owned not one, but two western saddles. But no one had ever taught me how to do it the right way. Within minutes it became apparent that there was a huge disconnect between me and this horse. I apologized and we retired to our respective corners.

The next time I rode him, I thought it would be best to tack him up English and go the way I was used to going. He had been advertised as "shown English and western", so there shouldn't have been a problem. But there was. Not a big one. He didn't throw a fit and buck me off. But the first time I rose in the stirrups to post the trot, his ears came up and he stopped dead, pitching me onto his neck. We kept at it, and gradually he stopped worrying so much about my rear leaving the saddle, but I had a suspicion that maybe English wasn't his native language.

This was confirmed not long after I bought him. I got an email from one of his past owners. The man had traced Dakota's registration to me and wanted to let me know that if I ever wanted to get rid of the horse, he would give the boy a permanent home. Laudable indeed.

I was beyond excited, not because I intended to send Dakota packing, but because I had the rare opportunity to find out the facts of the horse's background. If you think what the seller tells you is all there is, you're usually wrong.

What I learned was that the horse went western because he'd been wearing a western saddle from the get-go, not because he'd been trained to do a specific discipline. He hadn't been trained to do anything but go and stop. Any western pleasure showing he'd done had been with small children at schooling shows where staying on the horse and not running into the competition or the judge was sufficient for a ribbon. My sketchy understanding of western pleasure cues was not the entire reason for his seeming lack of interest in performing.

When I got to the "and they said he goes English" part, the man was taken aback. As far as he knew, the horse had never had an English saddle on his back prior to mine.

There's a moral to this story. I tried a horse that was advertised as performing in a discipline with which I was totally unfamiliar. Had I been a western pleasure show rider, I would have known in a few strides that this guy didn't have a clue. I didn't think to bring an English saddle because I trusted the seller to be honest (and knowledgeable—it's not always about dishonesty) about what the horse had done. If I'd ridden him in my own (English) style, I would also have noticed that he was not exactly on top of his game. That he was kind and gentle enough to let me flop around on him and "cue" him repeatedly without bucking me off (his former owner also mentioned that the horse had been a confirmed bucker!) was enough to make him a keeper, but a beginner would have been at a loss when Dakota came home and immediately "forgot" all his training.

If all of these warnings haven't dissuaded you, if you're headed out the door to put a deposit on that Perfect Schoolmaster you found on equine.com, congratulations and good luck. Read on. You're not out of the woods yet. The rest of you can go in peace, skip the rest of this book, and enjoy a long, happy life of bowling or collecting Precious Moments figurines. You with the checkbook, you're still mine.

Part Two:

So You Bought One Anyway…Now What?

Sometimes luck rides with the ignorant. I couldn't have predicted that I'd survive Zip's babyhood.

Chapter 12

What Horse Owners Need to Know, A Vet's-Eye View

Ah, the rural glory of a couple of pigmy goats and a horse or two flinging merrily about the barnyard..! If you haven't already taken the plunge into any kind of livestock ownership, there are a few points to consider before you buy something as big, expensive, and possibly dangerous as a horse.

I've been there. With many, many years around horses to my credit, I moved to the country and bought a horse. The mare was so ugly, it made my little daughter cry to look at it, but the horse was mine. What wasn't mine was the sense God gave a gopher. While Jess cried about my ugly new "cow", I stood in the aisle of the boarding barn crying because I thought I'd killed the beast. I knew all the tricks of the show pen, but I didn't know horses slept lying down.

With 48 years of experience now behind me, I'm still no expert, so when I wanted to write about what horse owners need to know, I called on someone who is. Dr. Fugaro* was the surgeon who had recently gelded my miniature stud. A veterinarian and a teacher, he seemed a good candidate to help me fill in the blanks. I am of the opinion that a lot of people who own horses probably shouldn't, at least not without some basic training.

This chapter may be the most important in the book for a novice owner, so take heed, take notes, highlight....there will be a quiz at the most inopportune time, and I won't be the one giving it! If you aren't willing to master what's in this chapter, you need to buy a goldfish and give up the horse thing once and for all.

My question to him was "What would you, as a vet, most like your clients to know?" His answer took two hours.

"First and foremost," the Good Doctor said without an instant's hesitation, "what I would say every horse owner has to have, but you can't teach it, is experience, and the more experience they've had the more comfort they have with [the horse]. With that being said and not being available, one, they need to know their horse … how to handle a horse and handle them well …

"What I mean by handling, they need to know that lovey-dovey horse that's in their back yard is not the same way when somebody is sticking a needle in them, and they need to treat them as such."

So let's start with your experience level. From the lowest experience level to the highest, rank yourself as follows:

1. I can tell a horse from a cow.
2. I have been in the company of a horse owned by someone else.
3. I have ridden a horse at least once.
4. I have taken riding lessons.
5. I have leased or borrowed a horse from someone for more than six months.
6. I have owned a horse.
7. I have worked at a boarding farm or other horse facility.
8. I am a riding instructor or farm manager.
9. I am an expert in the field of equine husbandry—vet, farrier, horse dentist, etc.
10. I am a horse.

If you score somewhere below 6, you probably need some additional training and hands-on experience before you tackle horse ownership. "We teach here [in Centenary College's Equine Studies program] all the time that these are not the horses that you stand behind and groom in bad positions," says Dr. Fugaro. "You've got to treat them like they're a wild animal and they're going to hurt you, and that's a big problem. There's a big liability for horse owners getting hurt while a vet is working."

Example? "Getting hit in the face with the twitch. Handling and restraint is a huge thing." For you beginners, a "twitch" isn't a dance variation. It's a chain or mechanical nose-cruncher that pinches a horse's nose to keep him contained while he's being worked on. Not pretty, but very effective. The handle of the twitch becomes a deadly weapon when the horse in question decides he's heading for parts unknown and swings his 40-pound head around to scope out the nearest exit. Handle meets human head, and *bam!*

"I would say that every owner should be able to do a physical exam. I think every owner should own a stethoscope as well as a pair of hoof testers. They don't have to be the most expensive; they can be the cheap ones. They should be able to get a heart rate, a respiratory rate, temperature ... and they should be familiar with their horse's feet, their gut sounds, and they should know that each horse is going to be different on those.

"The most common [horse] injuries are going to be colic, lacerations, eye injuries ... broken bones are not as common as you might think. The most common [lameness] is a foot abscess.

"Now that's where you're asking the owner to become a veterinarian. I don't expect them to be that. I expect them to be able to take one or two steps and at least be in communication with the vet."

Dr. Fugaro went on to say that while no one likes being awakened in the middle of the night, it's better for a vet to hear "I think Fuzzbutt might be colicking ..." as soon as the first symptoms are noticed than to get that call and hear, "Fuzzbutt is down and kicking and his eyes are rolled back into his head. How long? Oh, about six hours ..."

So, we can sum up the list as follows: Handling and basic first aid. That means experience. Where can you go to get it? My first choice would be a part-time job at a barn. Next on my list would be leasing a horse at a big lesson barn where there are plenty of people, including the horse's owner, to walk you through the basics. Riding lessons are great if they also include horse management. Few do.

In fact, here's another case-in-point. At a lesson/training/sale barn I frequented, I came upon a fellow owner who was afraid something was wrong with her horse. She asked me to look at him, and there was no question in my mind that this animal was in serious distress. The barn owner refused to help for various personal reasons having nothing to do with the horse's welfare, and unpaid vet bills had black-listed the place at many vets' offices. I gave the owner my vet's number, and the call was made, but not in time. Within a few days the horse had to be euthanized.

Here we had an owner trying to do the right thing. She had some experience with horses in her youth, but not enough. She was in a professional barn, but the barn owner was not behaving professionally. She called for help, but not trusting her instincts, she waited too long. All-in-all it was a bad finish from a fair start. Hindsight is great, but it's impossible to say which of the negative aspects of this deal was the killer. It was a conspiracy.

Dr. Fugaro says that many vets offer newsletters, and sometimes, particularly if you live near a vet school or large university with an animal

Joanne M. Friedman

science department, those would be good places to look for classes you can take. Volunteer at a handicapped riding center. Most offer instructor training, which is another great place to start learning how much you don't know.

Horse ownership is a full-time- total immersion experience. Start before the horse's feet hit the barnyard, and you'll be much better armed for the battles you'll be fighting.

[*Thanks to Dr. Michael Fugaro, VMD, Diplomate ACVS, graduate of University of Pennsylvania. Dr. Fugaro interned at University of Guelph and Purdue University, and is currently Associate Professor of Equine Studies at Centenary College in New Jersey]

Chapter 13

How Horses Think

We humans are cocky. We fully believe that it is our job to be in control of everything on the planet, and we devote ourselves entirely to that goal. We are able to ignore the evidence all around us, and when a little of it creeps in, we beat it with a stick until it's dead. So we have problems with the "lesser creatures" on the planet, the ones that we selfishly believe were put here as a "blessing" to us.

If we took one decent, open-minded look around, we'd have to admit that Nature Happens. Watch the weeds you battled to a draw last year come popping back despite all the power of human chemistry. Check out the rabbits visiting the all-you-can-eat buffet that was your veggie garden. Smack a few thousand mosquitoes or let a tick bury itself in your neck. Can you really imagine that humankind is in any way demonstrating our superiority? We're not ahead in this game. We're the kids with tape on our glasses and pocket protectors and a dull expression.

Yet we make animals captive, bring them into our lives, and expect them to toe (or hoof) the line. We treat them as we treat each other. We bully them, beat them, force them, and ignore their voices. Then we're surprised when Sparky bites the neighbor or Fuzz Butt dumps our special little spandex-covered rear in the mud and stalks off to spend quality time with her pasture mates. Go figure.

Against everyone's better judgment, you have bought a horse. Now what? We'll assume you've read Part One of this book instead of just skimming for the sexy parts. You've bought all the right stuff and you've found a place for your horse to live, hopefully where more level minds prevail. But the first time you go to the barn, you can't get Old Pie to look at you let alone let you catch him in the pasture. If you're as bad as I was, you can't even catch him in his stall. My first horse had a permanent headache, greeting me with a sigh and hindquarters turned in my direction every single day of the six months that I owned her. She knew we were wrong for each other when I simply could not see the manure for the sawdust. If that isn't a commentary on the superiority of humans, I don't know what is.

The good part about your novice status is that you may not yet have developed the bad habits that some more seasoned horse people have. You are a tabula rasa, a blank slate, upon which your horse can write reality without having to erase some human-centric fantasy first.

Let's begin with the fact that horses don't misbehave. They behave, period. If you don't like the behavior, you may feel you have the right to "correct" it in some quick and direct way. More and more often, thanks to excellent guidance and research available to all of us, we can see the behavior from the horse's perspective. Whatever he's doing, he's got what he thinks is a very good reason for it.

If you're honest, if you think about it from the horse's perspective, is our insistence that Super Widget learn the inside-leg-outside-rein cue any more comprehensible to him than his fear of squirrels and the resulting sideways dash across the arena is to us? Do you think he totally "gets" the fly-spray thing? Or the splint boots? Or the mane-pulling? Especially the mane-pulling!

Horses don't waste energy on annoying their human partners. Sure, there's the occasional horse with a great sense of humor who may do exactly that, but by the time you find yourself the butt of an equine joke, you will long since have learned how to listen. Horses don't play with people they don't trust, and they don't trust people who don't listen. Horses, being prey animals, conserve energy and use it to reach their primary goal, which is survival. They play with each other, which is as important to them as your social life is to you. They make friends; they share love. They enjoy a nice, sunny day. If you're good, you'll learn a lot from them. If you're great, you won't do any damage along the way.

If you are a typical beginner, you are more afraid of your horse than in love with him. Sure, you can handle him. You took lessons and led the school horses around without injuring yourself or them. You probably picked up more horse lore than you realize. The key to survival is to relax and understand that unless you are unnecessarily aggressive or causing him pain, your horse is not out to get you. If he bumps you and knocks you over, either he didn't see you, or he didn't care. The first is your problem. You need to always let your horse know where you are. The second is a training issue. If it happens all the time, one of you is in need of retraining by a professional.

The key to surviving horse life (besides the obvious need for a sugar daddy) is to think like a horse. Under no circumstances are you a part of his "herd". That is a concept that can only cause trouble in the long run. You are not a horse, so you're disqualified from the start. You don't speak the language, but you can (and must) learn at least its basics. You don't have a spot in the pasture, and you don't spend all day and all night with the horses. You are human, technically a predator to his prey persona, and you need to be in charge in order to avoid being hurt. He wants you to be in charge. He wants you to be the benevolent dictator who brings him food when he's hungry, supplies him with peace and safety. If you ask for cooperation in return, he'll be happy to oblige, but don't fall for the idea that horses play tit-for-tat like humans do. "He'll love me if I_____" can only get you into trouble. If he likes your smell and you treat him with respect and are consistent in your demands and rewards, he'll be fond of you. He'll work with you. There's some mystery as to why horses put up with us, but we're not asking the hard questions here.

The best way to approach a horse is with confidence. Old wives' tales about the predator/prey relationship that should be our natural state need to be revisited in light of current research. Unless your horse has witnessed you chasing down and killing something, he may not be completely aware of your omnivore status. Sure, he can smell meat on your breath, but he's judging you moment-by-moment based on your behavior. He wants safety and food, and you're his best bet for getting those easily. If you're not a total idiot who approaches him screaming and waving a whip, he's not going to be afraid of you. Even a foal is more curious than fearful unless you or Mommy give him reason to feel otherwise. Cautious curiosity is the basis of a horse's personality, and it's what makes it possible for you to train him. He wants to know what's up with that cookie in your pocket and the saddle in your hand. He needs to know. Learning what you want is what keeps him safe.

So the first thing you need to practice is self-assurance. Before you approach the horse, inhale, exhale, and relax. Then allow yourself to feel as if anything that happens will be within your ability to handle it. Believe it or not, if you're frightened, the odors and vibrations you give off that your horse can sense will scare him more than he scares you. A scared horse is a busy horse, and a busy horse is a dangerous horse. He's not thinking about you or your safety when he's worried that he's going to be attacked. Self-preservation is his middle name. You creep up to him with an attitude of fear and worry, and he's out the door.

Let's inspect the initial meeting as if we were watching you and Buzz Saw through the barn window. You, hesitant and a little hunched into your fear walk up to him slowly with your hand extended. He knows something's up because you're obviously terrified. He reacts with nervous energy. You'll see it in his eyes that suddenly look huge, his nostrils that flare and snort, and the ears that flick in your direction and stay there. That big snort that launched a snot rocket into your hair is his way of clearing his nasal passages so he can smell you better. He raises his head so he can see you clearly out of the bottom part of his eyeballs where close-up vision happens for horses. He screams to his friends, hoping for backup. From his perspective, he's got seconds to determine what kind of threat you pose. From yours, he has just grown three feet taller and gained weight, a behemoth about to rampage over you. This can't be good. It's easy to predict a rear, a rush past you, or some other escape maneuver that can cause you and your horse bodily harm.

Since this is a fantasy, you get a do-over.

This time you walk into the barn smiling and chatting pleasantly to your new horse, and Buzz Cut responds with curiosity. You're upright and moving smoothly, the way a human in control should move. Your actions are purposeful. Your expectation is that the horse will remain calm and even experience happiness at your sudden appearance in his day. You expect that if you walk past him, he will follow you with his eyes and probably get out of your way to give you room. If you've got a cookie pocketed, you ask him for something first (head down, back up, move your foot...whatever floats your boat), then give it to him. The end. His head never flies up in the air and his eyes and ears are relaxed because you haven't indicated that you are any kind of a threat or that one is imminent from somewhere nearby. Instead, you've allowed him to feel safe and experience curiosity. Now you're speaking horse!

Body language is everything for horses. The prey animal mentality precludes a lot of vocalization. We chatter constantly. Horses rarely talk to each other. A horse pasture is generally a very quiet place. If the ogre doesn't know you're there, he's not coming to eat you. That's just Nature at work.

Of course you're excited about your first horse, but he can tell excitement from panic. Just don't jump up and down until he's gotten to know you better.

Cautious curiosity is the horse's basic approach to life.

Chapter 14

What You Need to Do Right Away

I don't like the word "should" because it leads to misunderstanding and battling between horse and human partners. Instead, here is a list of behaviors that you can teach your horse that will make him a more pleasant companion, welcome at any boarding farm, and a fun buddy all around. Teach him (or at least don't un-teach him) to:

- Stand still when you want to catch him

- Not push, bump, shove, or bite you

- Not frisk you for treats

- Stand tied without pulling back or rearing

- Lead without rushing ahead or dragging behind you

- Stand still for grooming and tacking up

- Go through gates without rushing

- Move quietly and with respect for you whether you're on the ground or in the saddle

- Allow his feet to be handled

- Allow you to touch him all over, including head, ears, eyes, tail, and anyplace else you'd like for whatever reason (as long as you're polite about it)

Not too bad. If you were smart enough to take an experienced horse person with you when you bought this horse, he has probably already been trained to do all of these things. Your job, like it or not, is to avoid screwing him up.

The first rule of training is that intermittent reinforcement creates much stronger habit strength than continuous reinforcement. In English, that means that if you let him grab your sleeve with his teeth every now and then because you're distracted or it's cute in the moment, or you're texting your BFF and don't notice, he will become a confirmed sleeve-chewer faster and more effectively than if you gave him a cookie every time he did it and then quit the cookies entirely.

Like a small child, a horse is programmed to try to get what he wants until he's sure he can't or the attempts become painful. Your new horse Milo may want to prove he's tougher than you, or he may just enjoy the game. Regardless, grabbing your sleeve serves some purpose for him. If you never let him get away with it—if you yell at him, shake or pop the lead, make him turn in a circle, or in some other way indicate that the behavior is unacceptable—he will quit very quickly. If you always let him do it he'll continue until you completely stop allowing it. It will take time for him to quit after a bad start like that, but it will happen.

If, however, you sometimes let him do it, he'll have to keep trying indefinitely because he isn't clear on the rule you've made. "Hmmmm.... it's okay when she's wearing brown? When her boyfriend is visiting? When she smells like peanuts?" See what I mean? You would behave the same way if you had no clue what the rules were. You'd keep trying things until you figured it out, and that could take a very long time indeed!

This brings to mind visualization. If you can visualize what you want your horse to be like, and you can aim your behavior at that goal, his will follow. You want quiet, peaceful times with a well-mannered animal? Then that's what all of your behavior has to indicate.

Chapter 15

Reinforcement, Positive and Negative

Most people with or without horses are not clear on what the whole reinforcement thing is about. It took me four years of psychology school to get it, so don't feel embarrassed if you don't quite have it yet.

What psychologists call "positive reinforcement" is what the rest of us call "reward" or "payoff". You do something right and someone tells you it was right and gives you something you want. The payoff is used to encourage you to do the same thing again.

In horse terms it means catching the horse doing what you want him to do and telling him he got it right, then giving him something to convince him of the value of repeating the behavior. For instance, you want him to stand still while you comb his mane. He tends to fidget, which is frustrating. You pick a day to focus on that behavior, arm yourself with whatever treat works best for him, and set up the situation for his success. You start by making sure he's in a good mood and calm. Fuss over him. Groom him thoroughly so he's relaxed and happy. Then you take one small clump of mane in your hand and comb it through.

Since you've made all possible efforts to see to it that he'll still be quiet when you do that, he probably will be. Any horse can stand for one quick comb-stroke if he's already in The Zone. As soon as he does that, you make a fuss, give him his cookie, and quit for the day. Go riding or whatever you had planned to do. If you keep it up, working slowly toward your goal of his standing through an entire mane-combing experience, it will happen. It will happen more quickly if you incorporate clicker training, but for now you're doing great!

As you can see, there is nothing negative about this scenario. At no time did you punish the horse (you didn't, did you?), nor did you remove some sort of noxious stimulus in exchange for him doing what you asked. All positive all the way.

Positive reinforcement has all kinds of trendy new names, but in the end it's all the same old conditioning discovered eons ago by one B.F. Skinner and a bunch of lab rats. You show the horse what you want and pay him when he does it. It works for you; why wouldn't it work for him? Eventually you can stop the treats and he'll be happy with just petting and fussing. Some horses are happy with that right from the start. Research has indicated that young horses learn much faster with a food reward than without it. My own research has shown that old horses also learn more quickly for frosted mini-wheats than for a pat on the head. You make your own decision. Try it both ways and see how it goes. It's all good, all positive, and all natural, so it's hard to go wrong.

Negative reinforcement is a whole different ball game. In training circles it's often called "release" or "release from pressure". The process involves you introducing some sort of negative stimulus into the situation and waiting for the horse to do what he has to do to get away from it. When he does, the end of the negative is sufficient to keep him performing the same way over and over.

Revisiting the grooming lesson, we can introduce the negative by taking hold of the section of mane we want to comb and pulling on it with consistent (relatively hard) pressure. While we pull, we comb. If the horse pulls back, the pressure increases, so he is enticed to stop pulling so we'll stop pulling. The ending of all that pulling is his reward. We have shown him that we do not want him to pull away.

The failing of this process is that we've only told him one thing we do not want. That leaves a lot of leeway in terms of behaviors we might want. He may spend considerable time and energy trying out alternative behaviors before he hits on the one we actually wanted. And we have to be extremely attentive and sensitive to note exactly the instant when he shows that he is leaning toward doing that specific behavior. It's a little messy. It's the equivalent, in my opinion, of putting a child in a room with two other children and turning his chair so his back is toward them then stepping back. He feels the pressure to turn toward the others, so he tries. You turn him back again. He tries talking to them, and you move his chair farther away. He starts to fidget and you move his chair still farther away. He starts to cry, and you move him again. Eventually he puts his head down and falls into silence. Suddenly you jump up and hand him a cookie, tell him he's wonderful, and turn his chair to face the others'.

Of course he's done what you wanted, but he's also performed a series of other behaviors and might be at a loss as to which one you're thrilled with. He's also probably pretty upset and depressed. Since you can actually speak to him, it would have been simpler to tell him what you did want instead of what you didn't. It's a little harder when you can't use your words, but it's still do-able. Negative reinforcement—I'll stop pinching you as soon as you say "Uncle"—does work, but it is not the most efficient training method in the book.

[Enter the Big Paint Gelding]

Zip, as it turns out, is a very quick learner, and he learns no matter what method I use. Sometimes he learns what I'm trying to teach him. Sometimes he learns something I really wasn't counting on.

When he was younger, he was constantly creating troubling situations. In the pasture or in the barn, he was always voted Horse Most Likely to Earn a Beating. Of course I don't do beatings—we'll get to "punishment" in a minute—but negative reinforcement has been all the rage for a long time, so he's had his share of that.

The moment that comes quickly to mind involved a period of time when he simply didn't want to work. He would do it if pressed, but he wasn't going to make it easy to get him there. When you start with a baby horse, you see lots of developmental stages that other owners never experience. This was one of his worst. One day he was my Good Boy, merrily trotting around on command and listening with at least one ear to my commands. The next, he stood with his feet planted by the mounting block. He was willing to back up. That's all. Backing up had never been his favorite activity, so this was both a surprise and an annoyance.

Had I been more experienced in child-rearing, I would have been able, I'm sure, to pinpoint the cause of the change. Instead I spent days walking him backwards around the arena, stopping occasionally to check for forward willingness, then backing some more. The idea was that backing, being something he disliked, was a negative reinforcer, one which I would gladly discontinue the minute he showed any evidence that forward was back in the game.

Not once during that time did he seem to care that we were logging miles in reverse, so in an unaccustomed flash of brilliance, I thought, "Well, maybe he forgot he could go forward! Or maybe he thought reverse was what I was asking for!" Right. Well, sane or not, the solution I came up with was simple. I got off, put the longe line on him, and suggested that he move forward. At first there was no movement. We both stood there wondering what we were doing in the hot sun. But then without further ado, he walked forward. I gave him lots of cheers and let him stop when he was ready to rest. We did that a couple of times until he seemed to be content to walk around in the usual direction. I remounted, and off we went, forward and without further incident.

Okay, there was one further incident a few days later, but a repeat of the process ended that in minutes, and the problem was over. I'd love to think I actually understood what he was doing and thinking, but I'd be lying to suggest I had any clue. What I did worked for reasons I do not understand. What is obvious, however, is that positive reinforcement—letting him be good and giving him credit for it when he was—was far more effective than backing him endlessly around the arena—the negative reinforcer.

While we're on the subject, ground work is never wasted energy. Anything you do with your horse that does not result in yelling or injury, anything that ends with both of you happy and at peace, is a good thing. So let's take a close look at what ground work is and how you can make it work for you and your new best friend.

You may have noted a singular lack of attention to the third training modality: Punishment. As a rule, punishment doesn't work. If the horse refuses to stand tied and you beat him for that refusal, next time he'll also refuse to be caught in the pasture. Beat him for that, and he may escalate into punishing you for your stupidity. Many a crazy horse has been made that way by punishment.

Sure, there are moments when a swift smack is called for. Most of those involve a horse putting you or someone else in direct danger. It is, in my opinion, okay to smack a horse that is biting you. That may not be a popular stand, but I believe a well-timed warning shot can forestall major problems.

But long-term use of punishment for training purposes is pointless, dangerous, and cruel. Don't do it. Don't let anyone else do it to your horse. Everyone involved will just have to find a better way in one of the other two modalities.

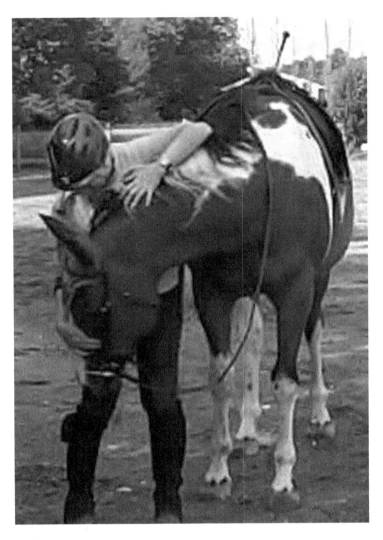

Always time for a hug while we work on ground manners

Chapter 16

Revisiting Ground Manners: When it's Time for a Reminder

At least once in the lifespan of any horse/human relationship there comes a moment when the balance shifts. The well-trained companion suddenly becomes a recalcitrant malcontent whose sole goal appears to be the complete irritation of his owner. The sudden shift can throw the horse owner into a panic of concern over the direction his horse life appears to be taking. What follows can range from depression to anxiety to anger and frustration to trading in Devil May Care for something with more horsepower and fewer brain cells.

The change, however, is anything but sudden. There are signs and clues that are sometimes missed in our overzealous efforts to excuse our animals' mistakes and cover up our own. Embarrassment is a horse person's worst enemy as it keeps him from seeing the field for the corn, so to speak.

The first clue may appear when the horse decides one day that he doesn't want to be caught. This minor rebellion is a test. If allowed to continue without consequences, the uncooperative behavior pattern will ramp up until someone gets hurt, someone gives up, or someone says stop in no uncertain terms. If Devil is allowed to get away with avoiding his owner in the pasture, if said owner follows him around for twenty minutes then shouts something rude and stalks off to find solace in the nearest bar, the next step may be pulling away when being led. Avoiding is annoying but not dangerous. Pulling can be a serious problem.

A horse that has been properly trained usually won't make a 180-degree turn-around overnight, so the first area that must be investigated (honestly, not with one eye closed) is whether or not there are holes in the training process that lead to the present situation. I don't necessarily mean that steps were skipped (though that's certainly a possibility). More often what has happened is that in the rush to move the colt from pasture puppy to saddle-broke while you're still young enough to ride him, some of the necessary bits were skimmed over. Not enough was demanded, too little was accepted, no consequences resulted from limit-testing behavior, and in the end the horse didn't actually learn the lesson being taught. He may have faked it or accomplished the requested task by accident, but he didn't buy into it.

Even more likely, there was a breakdown of communication between you. Truer words were never spoken that these: Be aware of what you are teaching! You may think you taught Slip Away to be caught, but you may have accidentally caused the opposite behavior. You approached one day not noticing another horse coming up behind you. He noticed and walked away. You, surprised, donned your Natural Horsemanship hat and chased him into running (negative reinforcement) in hopes that he would catch on to the fact that he'd have to work harder if he didn't let you catch him. Since he didn't read the same book you did, he didn't get that. What he got was that if he walked away, you would play tag with him. And if you did it long enough, when he quit there would be a cookie involved. What a great game!

Now, ten years and a bruised ego later, there is no getting around the necessity of revisiting the training process from the ground up.

Attitude is everything when it comes to horses. Theirs needs to be compliant, willing and focused. Yours needs to be firm, understanding, and include a cold-eyed look at your own abilities and inabilities. Barring veterinary issues, when a horse loses its ground manners, its owner had to have allowed that or caused it.

We begin, then, by first checking with the vet. A horse that doesn't want to be ridden because of a sore back, bad teeth, a soft-tissue injury that isn't making him obviously lame, will do what he can to avoid it. Many a horse, of course, will wait until you're in the saddle and headed off on a trail ride with eight of your most critical barn mates before he drops his head and bucks you off. That horse went from whispering (which you didn't hear) to yelling (which you felt immediately) without the intervening steps. This type of horse may be more unnerving to own than the one like Chatty Charlie who lets you know immediately when he's got a bug up his butt. Much as you might tire of his endless complaints, at least Charlie is keeping you in the loop and giving you a chance to right the wrong before he feels the need to ramp up his grievance process.

With all our ducks in a row and an attitude that will ensure success, we can begin to analyze each of the ground manners issues we're encountering and deal with them one at a time. The game is not lost, but the rules need to be tightened a bit. A well-trained and cooperative horse is a joy to be around and safe for everyone who has to deal with him. It's never too late to fill the gaps and recreate that companion you thought you had. View this process as a challenge and part and parcel of the equestrian experience, not as a failure for you or your horse. Remember that every time you approach your horse you teach him something. It's time to focus that education on what matters most.

As Mark Rashid has said many times, both human and horse need to be "soft", flexible, kind, and cooperative. The horse looks to the human for instructions. Miss the moment, and "soft" can turn hard and argumentative, not because the horse is that way, but because we humans don't know any other way to respond. Become pushy and forceful, and you risk losing the horse's trust. Horses truly do not lie. We might not like their answers to our questions, but they won't make up stuff like aliens stealing their homework. They will give the best answer they have to the questions we ask, and it's up to us not to assume the worst and overreact. Avoid that moment; give the horse the benefit of the doubt. But do not under any circumstances reinforce behavior that will present a danger to you, your horse, or anyone else. Don't punish, but don't reward. You can't make him love you by encouraging him to walk all over you.

Chapter 17

A Biting Remark

Horse owners have plenty of equine vices to be concerned about. Most habitual behaviors take more of a toll on the horse, the stable and the owner's nerves than on the owner. Stall-walking, cribbing, weaving, pawing, kicking the stall walls at feeding time and the other idiosyncrasies horses develop over time are generally related to too much confinement, boredom, or a sense of humor simply not appreciated by the humans in the horse's world. My horses have now all taught each other to lick the stall doorjamb after a grain feeding. They also all—including the mini who has to stand on tip-toe to do it—remove their halters and leads from the hooks next to their doors and throw them into the middle of the aisle each morning in a kind of equine roll call.

But the minor vices don't hold a candle to the Big Three:

1. Biting
2. Kicking
3. Charging

Biting is at the top of the list because it is insidious, difficult to cure, and very dangerous to everyone working around the horse.

In the horse world, biting is a way of dominating herd mates. Most horses respond well to each other's body language, so outright attacks are relatively unnecessary. Horses are far more attuned to minuscule movements and body positions than are humans, and they understand herd dynamics. Stallions will bite mares during breeding and other stallions during a fight for control of the herd. Mares will bite each other when there's a question of who stole whose boyfriend. They will occasionally bite their offspring if there's good reason for that strong a reprimand.

But some horses learn early on that humans are easily frightened and that control can be wrested away from them by a show of teeth. It may start as a nip on the shoulder or side when the girth is too tight or saddle fit is poor and causing pain. It may start as a means of getting attention. The horse who sticks his head over his stall door and reaches out for you as you pass may accidentally grab your shirt once. If you stop and talk to him, he may grab more than your shirt the next time. It may result from a battle—real or perceived—over personal space. Some horses have learned not to trust strangers and are not happy when one pokes his body into the stall without invitation.

Sometimes it's accidental. One of my favorite horse stories involves a friend who was hanging out with her horse in the pasture and didn't notice a rival mare approaching from behind her. Her horse, figuring the herd mate was out to grab his cookies, reached around and snapped. Unfortunately his owner's butt was between him and his target and firmly in the blind spot directly in front of his face. She sported a horse-mouth shaped wound for weeks.

Accidental bitings generally reflect a human lack of good judgment. Those don't often recur. It's the aggressive biter who is most dangerous, and that is the most difficult type of biting to cure.

Rule number one would have to be Don't Buy a Horse that Bites. Barring that, the next rule has to be Don't Put Yourself in Harm's Way. If you know your horse has developed a penchant for the taste of polyester, train him to stand cross-tied and always tie him firmly before you start grooming or tacking up. Eventually he will give up the habit on his own.

If he is an aisle-way attacker, find a way to close up the top of his stall. Stall screens are available, and many barn owners will be pleased to allow you to mount one if it means less bloodshed and fewer barn hands quitting due to injury. If he bites when you try to catch him in the pasture, don't do that. Run him into an enclosed space or have him left in his stall when you want to ride.

The electronic training collar works wonders for biting. My mini stallion is now convinced that his herd mates all have electric hindquarters, and he avoids them instead of taking chunks. Though no one actually likes the thought of hitting a horse, a well-timed and swiftly-delivered smack with a crop will sometimes be enough to convince the biter you are not to be messed with. It is not true that hitting a horse on the nose will make him head-shy. If it were, my youngest would require anesthesia for bridling. He doesn't bite anymore. In fact he approaches a hand-fed treat with his "gentle" mouth—

wide-open, tongue thrusting, and eyes closed. No harm, no foul. The trick with any kind of punishment is to keep your anger at bay. This is not about revenge; it's about training.

The aggressive vices are not something to be treated lightly. If you cannot find a way to prevent or cure biting on your own, don't hesitate to call a respected professional. The life you save may be your own.

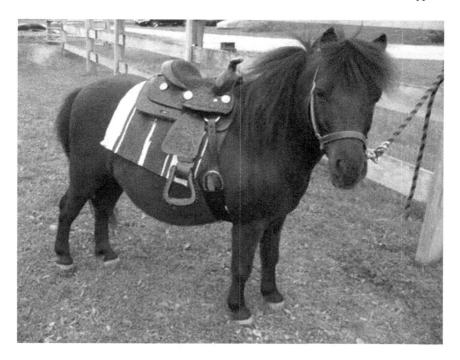

Standing tied is an essential skill.

Chapter 18

Reforming the Puller

So, your horse, which has already been vet-checked and had his teeth floated and his feet trimmed, avoided you in the pasture, and now as you lead him into the barn he has attempted to pull the lead through your hands. How quick are you? If you're alert enough, you may be able to plant your feet and throw your weight onto the lead with enough sharp force to startle him into stopping. If you're not paying attention or not physically up to a tug-of-war with a 1200-pound teenager, the best thing to do is let go of the lead. Unless he's going to be heading out into traffic, don't fight him. You're already off-balance. He's not. Let him run. If he has access to a pasture, you'll just have to follow him until he steps on the lead and stops himself or tires of the game. He probably won't injure himself. Self-preservation is a horse's strongest instinct. If he does manage some sort of injury, there's nothing you can do to stop him. He outweighs you. You can't fight a horse on his own turf.

One way or another, you will finally regain some sort of control over the animal, even if it means letting him run into his stall and closing the door behind him. My occasional forays into this area with Zips Money Pit generally end with him wrapping the lead rope around a fence post and stopping, tied. I will admit to enjoying the look of startled awe on his face when he sees me fifty or a hundred feet away and he neatly tied to the fence. "How did you *do* that?!" It lends a little street cred to my trainer persona.

What you do next will determine how far this game will go. Leave him penned up for a bit while you prepare for the next step. Begin by putting a stud chain on your lead. They are readily available at tack shops for a few dollars. When you next approach Whiz Bang, run the chain through the ring on the near (his left) side of the halter, wrap it once or twice over the noseband so that it isn't hanging loosely against his nose, and clip it to the off (his right) side ring. Give one short (gentle!) tug before you try to lead him so he'll be forewarned that there's something new afoot. We're not out to trick him, just to help him understand what it is we want.

You are not going to slam him around and embed that chain in his nose. It's there as a second-level warning. If you have a clicker and some small treats (frosted shredded wheat minis are great for this), start by asking him nicely to walk with you. If he does, click-treat. If he doesn't, however, you must react instantly. A verbal pre-cue—whoa is a good one, but you can make up your own (just keep it clean in case the kids are nearby)—should precede by at least two or three seconds any pressure on the lead rope. If he doesn't respond, tighten your grip and pop once, twice, three times, gently! Three is key. As I recently learned at a clinic, in the horse's mind one cue can be a mistake, so he ignores it. Two gets his attention. On three he's sure you're talking to him. Again, you're not beating on him with the chain. That is counter-productive and will piss him off. He's still bigger and heavier than you are; never forget that for a minute.

If on the third pop he is still moving and you're beginning to slide, dig in hard and yank his head around. If you need more leverage, dally the rope around a pole or a tree, but don't give up. The minute he stops and looks at you without moving his feet, click-treat or pat him and tell him he's good. Release the pressure on the lead immediately. This first retraining lesson has to be a strong one, but it's a lesson, not a punishment.

How often you will have to repeat this will depend on how religiously consistent you are. You are setting a small, specific goal. You want him to walk without pulling. You have defined what that means, and you have showed him with a reward that he can accomplish the task. No matter how deeply ingrained the behavior may be, he will, over time, see the point in changing it. Depending on how good you are with all of your other work with this horse, he may give in quickly or he may continue to test you for years. The more often you fail to respond quickly and consistently, the more he will test you.

When at last he has stopped testing, get rid of the chain and reward him for his efforts as consistently as you reminded him when he was wrong. He may still need a tune-up from time to time, but you should see an immediate improvement in your relationship. Horses are herd animals and totally understand the collective need for comfort and security in the huge game of Follow the Leader that is herd life. Be a good leader so he can be a good follower.

Chapter 19

Cribbing: Why, How, and How Not to Stop It

If there's one thing that will strike fear into the heart of a barn manager and keep you and your horse homeless, it's the words, "Oh, and by the way ... he cribs a little". For those of you who have never encountered this particular vice, "cribbing" is related to wood-chewing and wind-sucking and can encompass both of those habits as well. The "cribber" grabs the top rail of the fence (or any other horizontal surface he can wrap his rapidly-deteriorating teeth around) and pulls back slightly. That's basic cribbing. If he gulps air into his gullet at the same time, he's also a wind-sucker. If when he walks away, there's a hunk of wood missing from the fence, he's a wood-chewer as well.

None of these is a good thing for the horse or for his environs. Barn owners hate cribbers because their teeth take a toll on the barn and the fencing. Horse dentists and vets hate cribbing because it wears down the cribbing horse's teeth and causes him to lose weight because he'd rather crib on his bucket than eat his grain. Over the long term, a severe cribber may stop eating. His teeth will wear away, and he will begin to live for the endorphin rush of his addiction. Horse people avoid buying cribbers because of the long-term veterinary issues (and the homelessness thing), and other boarders may well form a posse and attack the barn manager if a cribber is stabled near their otherwise-healthy horses. Though recent research suggested that horses do not learn from each other, I have seen it happen over and over. I won't stand on the platform that they can't, though there's only anecdotal information that suggests that they can.

In my own little herd, Zip's mom, Pokey, developed the habit of licking her stall's doorframe after she eats. When Zip was old enough to be in his own stall, he did the same thing. Genetics? I think not, though researchers are looking at the possibility that related horses might also share a dietary imbalance. I bought Dakota, a then-fourteen-year-old gelding, four years ago. He had his own vice, but it wasn't that one. Guess what he does now? I've seen one of my mares teach the other horses how to open the latches on their stall doors. Zip learned to use a broom to "sweep" in front of his stall for cookies, a trick he learned by watching the barn slaves. Dakota does it now as well. If that's not evidence of training going on among the horses, then I'm an Appy's Aunt Ada. Most horse owners who are sensibly paranoid and like their horses healthy, won't stable next to a cribber.

Can cribbing be cured? This is a subject that is debated constantly. The traditional solutions involve putting a muzzle on the horse to keep his teeth off the things he likes to chew, or use of a cribbing collar. The collar, usually resembling a nutcracker with leather straps attached, fits around the horse's throat in such as way as to prevent him from making the gulping motion that allows the air to enter. Keeping the horse in a stall that does not afford him any place to grasp with his teeth is a good plan, but virtually impossible. The edge of his feed bucket is more than enough to allow him to maintain this habit.

A more recent innovation, and one which I've found successful for vices like attempted murder of full-sized horses by a mini stallion, is the electronic training collar I already touched on in the last chapter. This is the same basic device in common use on dogs for many years to stop them from ravaging the countryside. The collar is relatively painless for the horse to wear and the amount of electricity generated is very small. At a low setting, it's nearly imperceptible to a human hand. I tested it on my own hand, and I am certainly not a stoic. Demonstrations have shown a horse cured of cribbing, stall-walking, weaving, and other vices in only one or two experiences with the collar. The point of the jolt isn't to punish the horse, and it's important that anyone trying this method understand that and start at the lowest effective setting. To paraphrase Mark Rashid, do only as much as you have to, but be willing to do what you can. Cribbing is an addiction, a vice usually brought on (as are most vices) by boredom and too much time spent confined in a stall (and possibly nutrients missing from feeding regimens, but that's just a current guess being bandied about). Confinement causes stress. Humans under stress will smoke, drink, and chew their nails. Horses weave, stall-walk, crib and bite. These are all different reactions to the same situation. The jolt of the electronic collar simply breaks the cycle like the snap of a rubber band on a smoker's wrist. If the cycle is broken consistently for a short period of time, and the training is reinforced if needed later on, the habit can be successfully broken.

Of course the best approach is to avoid putting horses in stressful situations in the first place. More and more research is being done on the subject of how we damage our horses physically and mentally with our careful stabling and avoidance of anything approaching a natural lifestyle. Right now the Farnum Company, makers of many horse products including supplements and vaccines, is engaged in research to determine if the stress we are inflicting on our horses is what is causing the increase in diseases and the increasing failure rate of vaccines and medications.

Avoidance of problems before the fact is generally better than a cure after the fact.

Chapter 20

The Reluctant Bather

A recent article in Horse and Rider reported that research has determined that "vices" are not actually bad habits, but are psycho-social behavior patterns caused by lack of turnout and a dearth of equine companionship. In many cases, that is the case. Stall-walking, weaving, digging, kicking at the stall walls, aggression against anyone who dares enter the stall, and early cribbing certainly fall into the category of habits that would never have begun had the horse been living a life a little closer to what nature intended. Just to clarify, all horses should have ample pasture turnout time and horse friends with whom to share it. If they are given those things from the start, most of the behaviors we call "vices" would never occur to them.

I'm reminded of a thoroughbred stallion at a barn where I boarded and worked. The barn had no turnout suitable for a horse with his "manhood" intact, so he was permanently stall-bound. I remember him most vividly the day the barn owner took him from his stall for all of us to ride and play with. What was most striking was his height. In the stall he was short. He had dug a hole deep enough to make a nice dry well should the need arise, and he stood up to his knees in the hole giving the appearance of being maybe 15 hands high. When he strode up out of his stall, I was astounded! He was immense! Well over 17 hands and built with endurance in mind.

There was nothing wrong with this big boy. We all had a marvelous time riding him around the indoor longe pen, ducking to keep from hitting our heads on the rafters. He was sane and reasonable and not in the least dangerous. But forced to live in a stall without any reprieve, he had taken on habits that were unpleasant at best. Digging was the worst of them. Had he been allowed sufficient turnout time (even maximum-security prisoners get a daily hour in the yard!), he probably would have been much happier. He was thin and quiet. A lovely boy in need of a change of venue. His manners were exquisite but his vices were the pits…literally.

I shared that story to differentiate between vices and bad manners. Ground manners—the rules we teach our horses in order for us to be safe handling them and for them to be safe in our presence—are training issues. So far we've discussed the horse that pulls away from you when you're leading him and the one who stands on you while you're grooming. We've also talked about biting and cribbing. Of those behaviors, cribbing is the one most likely to have been born of boredom and the stress of an unnatural lifestyle without sufficient equine companionship. All of these are perpetuated, however, by owners who either inadvertently reward or simply miss the opportunity to break these habits. As Dr. Phil has said repeatedly, "we do what works". So do horses. Often the cause of the behavior is long gone, but the behavior persists because it has developed habit strength due to random reinforcement over months or years. Any behavior that is self-reinforcing is incredibly difficult to change since removing the reinforcer is not an option.

Avoiding bath time certainly falls into the "bad habit" category of ground manners. The initial cause is usually easy to tag. If you've had the horse forever, then you somehow contributed to the problem and can probably peg where you went wrong if you think about it honestly. If the horse is new to you, then the behavior issue probably stems from something earlier owners did, and you may be hard-pressed to figure out what that might have been. But laying blame serves no good purpose while analyzing the behavior can give you some leverage.

If he's refusing to walk into the wash stall or outdoor wash rack, he may never have been in one before. Many owners simply hose their horses off while holding them on a lead. Try that with your horse to determine if confinement or unfamiliar surroundings might be the issue. Be prepared to give a little to get a lot. If he backs away from you when the spray touches him, let him back up. You walk forward and keep the spray aimed at his feet, legs and chest. Eventually either he'll stop and stand or you'll tip to other behaviors that will give you a clue as to what's on his squirrelly little mind.

For instance, he may simply not like the spray—either its intensity or the sound. Try different nozzles on the hose. Try the hose without any nozzle and just a small stream of water. If all else fails, put the water in a bucket and try a sponge.

The key is to identify what, exactly, constitutes a bath. The hardest part of any training is separating both the behavior you're eliciting (and the one you hope to elicit) and the situation into their concomitant parts. On the situational side of bath time, you've got water, hose, intensity of the spray, temperature of the water, location, confinement, noise level, the presence (or absence) of other horses, and mood—both yours and his—among other factors. On the behavioral side you have fidgeting, fussing, biting, rearing, pulling away, pawing, shrieking for someone in the herd to come and save him, and whatever unique reactions your horse may invent. On the environmental side, you have the size, location, and even color of the wash stall or rack and the view from that position. That's a lot to contend with, so this is not going to necessarily be a one-shot repair.

The simplest and most effective approach to solving a problem like this one is to start from scratch. Pretend that your horse has never been bathed before and think about how you would introduce him to that activity. Don't begin in the cross ties in a wash stall if you're not sure he's ever been there. Begin on the lead with a sponge and a bucket of warm water. Make the process logical. Once you're sure he's okay with the water, the sponge, and the level of confinement of the lead, move to the cross-ties. Or if there is no wash stall or wash rack available, move to the hose without a nozzle, pointing it at his feet and legs first to judge his reaction before moving to his body. Watch his reactions. Back off before he has time to get really upset if you sense he's frightened.

Old Squeamish may never learn to love a bath—some horses just don't—but he can learn to stand patiently while you work efficiently and politely to get him de-skuzzed. Be matter-of-fact and firm, not aggressive. If you are circumspect and overly cautious, he'll begin to think there's something dangerous in the situation. That may be where you went wrong in the first place. Being alert doesn't mean being shy and frightened.

Try to make bath time fun. My big Paint is my least happy bather, but at the end of each bath he gets to use his nose to block the spray so I get wet. I make a big fuss over a little water, and he is thrilled.

Take your time. If you can only clean one leg, then do that. If he gets upset after half his body is done, move on to some other fun activity for a moment (work on his bow, for instance) and come back to bathing. Use the clicker to reinforce him for standing still. Make that the focus of the lesson so he'll forget about his bath phobia. Just don't ever let him decide he can intimidate you into quitting, or you'll have much bigger problems later on.

Well-trained horses are a joy to everyone.

Chapter 21

Baby Steps--
Task Analysis and Horse Sense

A horse trainer can spend many an hour in the pasture being with his animal, communing with him, and trying to imagine what horse-ness must feel like and still get nowhere fast with his attempts to alter the horse's behavior. All the Natural Horsemanship videos and books and magazine articles in the world won't help if the trainer has not mastered task analysis—the breaking down of a desired behavioral result into its parts. Spend all day yelling at Happy Fuzzbutt to move his hindquarters under him and you'll have a very amused horse and neighbors who are hoping their video of your antics will win them a big prize on TV. Fuzzbutt's hindquarters will be firmly where he wants them to be, stretched out behind him in all their glory. Pick up the inside rein, apply your leg; hum a Bach concerto, and nothing will change.

First understand that you are a horse trainer. Just as you inadvertently taught your kids to curse, you teach your horse something every time you interact with him. That makes you a trainer. That also makes you responsible for most of his behavior, good and bad.

It's important, then, to have a goal all the time so that what the horse learns is what you intended to teach him. The goal can be very simple: You want your horse to stand still while you brush him. The target behavior is the standing still. An analysis of the goal tells us that there is more here than meets the eye. What you're really asking the horse to do is:

1. Walk quietly on the lead to the spot you've chosen for the affair
2. Stop walking when you get to that spot
3. Accept standing tied for a period of time
4. Not move his feet while you're touching him

5. Not shift his hindquarters away from you
6. Not shift his hindquarters toward you
7. Not nip at your hindquarters while your back is turned
8. Not frisk you for treats when you are working on his head

More complex than you thought? It gets worse. Each of those individual behaviors has a subset of its own. Walking quietly to the grooming area without running you down involves his respecting your space and your person and knowing that you want him to stand still in a particular spot. Accepting standing tied means he has to have learned that you are not a threat and that he will be freed eventually, and so on.

Does this mean that every time you want to ride old Fuzzbutt you have to go through a lengthy training process? Of course not. If it did, I'd be playing golf instead of learning dressage. What it does mean is that the fact that your horse stood quietly once does not necessarily mean he'll do it every time unless all of the behaviors leading to that goal have been successfully mastered. Some horses are quicker to learn than others. Some are intuitive enough to figure out what you want and what they'll get if they cooperate. Some just like people and will do whatever they can to please.

Task analysis is most important when you are faced with an animal who is not cooperative or whose basic training is a little sketchy. It's also vital when you are trying to teach a brand-new behavior that is not natural to horses, like a trick or a complex pattern of actions such as the movements of classical dressage. Something as obvious as getting the horse to side-step with his back end as a precursor to spinning or doing turns on the forehand requires that you recognize that there is a first step and start there.

This is where clicker training really shines, but let's look at even the clicker process as a series of tasks. You want to use the clicker to help the horse identify correct answers to your requests. You stand the horse in the cross-ties, point the whip at his foot and say, "Pick it up". He does, because he's used to doing that for you when he hears those words, and you click. The sound scares the wits out of him, he rears, breaks the ties, and you've got a whole new training project.

What would have worked better would have been an explanation, in horse terms, of the clicker thing. Clicking it nearby a few dozen times so he gets used to the sound is step one. Picking a simple targeting task like touching your crop with his nose so that you can click and treat is the second step. Once he's got the idea that every click will be followed by a reward, the rest follows as the night the day. Before you know it, he's learning pretty much anything you can think of to teach him ... as long as you break it down into individual tasks.

Task analysis is the key to every training program for horse and for rider. Become an ace at breaking down behaviors into the parts that comprise them, and you'll be on your way to a better horsemanship all around.

Chapter 22

For the Record: Organizing Your Horse Life

When asked what horse owners need to know, New Jersey veterinary surgeon Michael Fugaro, VMD, was adamant about several things. The horse owner's ability to produce rational answers to questions certainly sat close to the top of the list. "The typical story is, 'Has your horse been vaccinated?' … 'Sure, Doc! He's gotten everything.' Well, what's everything? What your veterinarian may treat with is different than somebody in the Northwest." It's the gaps that can kill a horse.

[Enter the miniature stallion from the Backyard Breeder…]

Everyone has a story about someone else who isn't up to snuff. I try not to be hypercritical, but when it comes to some things, I have to put my schoolteacher hat on and make a few red marks on some final essays. I have nothing bad to say about the young girl who sold me this horse. First, I had no right to buy a horse of a type I'd never dealt with. There, I've said it! I screw up royally when I get cocky. Had I known how different miniature horses are from the full-sized variety, I'd have run screaming instead of begging the owner to take my check. Oh, he's a wonderful guy and a great addition to the herd, but there were lots of lumps and bumps (mostly on the big horses and a few on me) along the way to getting to that point.

But this isn't about acclimating odd horses to the herd. This is about record-keeping. Whenever you buy a horse, you should always be given a copy of his health records. If you own a horse, you should keep a folder or something somewhere with a list of the important things. A file folder full of vet receipts will do if the receipts are detailed so you know what shots were given when.

The average horse requires at least two sets of vaccinations each year, including rabies and a list of shots targeted to whatever diseases are prevalent in your area plus the basics like Rhinopneumonitis and flu. An unvaccinated horse is at risk, but so are the vaccinated horses he comes into contact with. No vaccine is 100% effective, so an unvaccinated horse can easily become a carrier and infect a weakened horse even though that animal has already had his shots.

Knowing all this and with many years of experience behind me, I naturally asked for the records. The seller happily obliged. It was easy for her. The horse hadn't had any shots except for his "baby shots" seven years earlier and a rabies shot every three years, same as her dog. Since I wasn't expecting that level of ignorance from a breeder and experienced horse owner, I showed up with my trailer and no option but to bring the horse home and quarantine him until my own vet could give him whatever vaccinations he needed.

Let me hammer home that rabies is not nearly all the shots a horse needs, and he needs them sometimes a couple of times a year. At least she had a record of what had been done to him. A twelve-year-old pony came into the herd a few years earlier with ample shot records but without ever having seen a dentist. The loose tooth hanging in his gum was a good explanation for his problem with the bit. Duh! That owner gave us the vet's number and permission to call for the pony's history. That was fine since there was no emergency and we used the same vet. But handy records are a plus.

Sure, your vet's office is a fine fall-back position. They generally keep all of their clients' specifics in computer files and sometimes as hard copies as well, but when you've called the vet at 3 AM because Donut Hole is down and thrashing, odds are the vet's staff (who may also be his spouse) is still asleep, and the vet is not going to show up with a printout of the past five years of your horse's medical history. If you change vets or have to call the covering vet service in an emergency, those records won't be available at all.

It's up to you as the horse's owner to keep track of what your horse has been up to. There are lots of easy ways to do this, most requiring only the commitment on your part to avoiding standing around with a flashlight and a dumb expression while the vet asks questions you can't answer.

> Computer Software

Any software program that allows you to set up a database or spreadsheet will do. Most computers come with one. Microsoft loads PC's with Works or Office, and either will suffice for a basic chart of the what's, when's and why's of Donut Hole's life. In addition, there are programs made specifically for horse owners. Do a search online and see what's new and available at a reasonable price. I'm not a MAC owner, but I'd guess there's a similar load of stuff on your iBook.

You do, however, need to actually enter the information. For me, this is sometimes the sticking point. The remembering thing can be a bugger, so reward yourself when you do remember. Print out hard copies regularly. Computers crash almost as often as horses do.

> File Folders

Even if you have software, file folders are a great back-up plan. Envelopes are even better as the papers are less likely to fall out as you grab the records and dash out the door or plop them on the barn manager's desk. My system seems to work. I deposit the detailed receipt for whatever has just been done to my horse/horses on my desk in front of my monitor where I can't miss it. Eventually I remember to input the information into the computer. Once that's done, the paper goes into a file folder labeled "Horses" which resides in reasonably alphabetical order in a file cabinet next to my desk.

If I have a specific horse with a specific issue, I also have a specific envelope. That's especially important for my boarder's horse, as I need to be able to quickly sort his paperwork from the general collection.

> PDA (Blackberry, etc)

If you're really good about keeping techie items charged and ready, and you use your electronic data organizer often enough to know how to quickly access the files you've stored there, then this will work for you. Keep your horse's data updated on your computer, and periodically back it up onto your hand-held device. When you grab your coat for that trip to the barn, grab the PDA as well, and you'll be ready to answer all the questions the vet might ask and do so with the authority of a true organizational wizard.

If, on the other hand, your PDA is often sitting uncharged and untouched for weeks or months, or you commonly use it only to store phone numbers, five minutes before the vet arrives to determine why Cream Puff is sitting on his haunches humming "Bess, You Is My Woman Now" is not the time for a crash course in the finer points of information management. Grab the file folder or envelope with all the papers in it, and run.

➢ USB or "Thumb" drive

Unless you're a PC and your vet is a MAC, you can easily transfer all of your records (the ones you've been so diligently keeping in Word or Works or some other generic word processor) from your personal computer onto a tiny external drive that plugs into the USB port of your computer. Once it's there, you download the files onto it and unplug it. Many come with lanyards or belt clips or key rings attached for safe carrying and storage. It might work to have one with a key ring that holds your tack trunk key so you'll be sure to always have it with you. Few vets nowadays travel without a laptop computer, so it's easy enough for him to plug your little drive into his unit and look at what you've got there.

Just be careful not to mix the nude photos of your significant other with the horse files. The relationship with your equine professionals must remain unsullied.

Don't forget to periodically reorganize and update your information. You can throw away papers on a horse that has died. That's my general rule. Anything else stays on file for at least two years, and any documentation of a surgery or other drastic treatment remains indefinitely if only for date reference. When you sell or give away a horse, hand over the folder too. There's nothing more upsetting than buying a horse and having a problem with no idea whether or not this is something that's been addressed in the past. As a seller, there's no law saying you have to produce anything more interesting than a hand-written bill of sale, but we in the horse business need to pull together and clean up our approach to horse dealing. It might as well start with you.

Getting started with organization always seems daunting, but it's less so if you simply start today with whatever paperwork you have handy. Don't waste time kicking yourself over missing receipts or forgotten data. When you have time, call the vet's office and see if you can't sweet-talk someone into making a printout of your account history. That's a start. Save the receipts from your wormer purchases and note the date of administration on them. Save the farrier's bills, too. And the dentist's. You can save the receipts for your Valium and Xanax refills, but no one will be interested. Start today and tomorrow will be a better horse day all around.

Chapter 23

Vet Talk:
Give Your Horse a Physical

In interviews with Drs. Fugaro and Fazio, a single theme was recurrent: *Know Your Horse.* There are several levels on which the horse owner can apply that admonition. On the simplest level, it helps to be able to identify your own horse in a pasture full of other horses. Ridiculous? Not if you've had your horse groomed and ridden by another horse owner who couldn't tell yours from hers. If you have to take pictures and keep them on your fridge, then so be it, but you should know all the basics about your horse—color, age, size, markings, breed, sex…name.

Moving to a higher level, it's equally important to know your horse's personality. It's impossible to tell when a horse is sick if you don't know what he's like when he's well. Spend time with the horse. This is particularly crucial for non-horsy parents of horse-fanatic children. It's vital that you spend a few hours now and then interacting with the horse in your life. Children love their horses, but they are not always as astute as adults at noticing subtle changes or guessing what they might mean. If Lulu has been chipper and zippy for two years and suddenly becomes sullen and nasty, it's safe to bet that there's something amiss.

Things do go wrong with horses, and many of them require the services of a horse professional. If the horse is walking funny, the horseshoer might be the best person to call. If he's refusing to walk at all or isn't eating or has bucked little Suzy off three times in the past ten minutes, a vet check might be in order.

Let's say you go to the barn and find that Lulu is standing in her stall looking a lot like your elderly Aunt Mabel instead of the perky little filly you know and love. Her head is hanging, her lips flapping loosely, her eyes half-closed, and her feed untouched. Can you tell just by looking whether or not the horse is ill? You may be suspicious, but in order to be sure, you need to be able to do a basic physical examination.

Had I been more experienced, I would not have panicked over that sleeping mare because I would have known that she was prone to being prone during her nap time. Like their owners, horses have moods and habits that are often incomprehensible to everyone around them.

Dr. Fugaro says that all horse owners should have the basic tools at hand. He recommends a thermometer (the digital kind that you can buy for a few dollars at the supermarket will work just fine), a stethoscope (available very inexpensively from the farm supply store or any horse equipment catalog), and hoof testers. Weight tapes are very easy to come by for free from most feed companies or for a couple of dollars at the tack shop and should be in your first aid kit. It's not necessary to break the bank on this project, but with those few instruments and some clear-eyed assessment, an owner can make a far better judgment as to the relative health of her animal.

Long before Lulu first shows signs of illness, you should make up a note card with the following information:

✓ Age
✓ Weight
✓ Normal resting heart rate
✓ Normal resting respiration (breathing) rate
✓ Normal resting temperature (Use Vaseline to lubricate the thermometer and don't let it slip inside the horse!)

Do two or three assessments over a period of a couple of weeks and take the average readings for heart rate, respiration and temperature. Write all of this on a note card, laminate it (clear packing tape does a fine job) and stick it in your first aid kit or tack box—somewhere handy and near the horse for reference when you most need it.

When you finally do arrive to find Lulu suffering from some mysterious equine malady, pull out the card and a dry-erase marker and note:

✓ Her current weight (changes can be a sign of illness), her current heart rate, respiration, and temperature, and any other notable changes in her appearance.

✓ If her eyes or nose are running, write that down.

✓ Do a capillary refill test by lifting her upper lip and pressing her gum hard for a few seconds with your finger. The gum should go pale and then turn pink again very quickly. If you can time this with the cheap stopwatch you also stuck in your kit, so much the better. If the pink color doesn't return quickly (or at all) note that.

✓ If her eyes are glassy or appear irritated, note that.

✓ If her breathing sounds ragged or she's coughing, make a note.

✓ If she appears listless or can't move, make a note.

✓ If she refuses to take a step forward or is standing in an odd position, bring out the hoof testers, pick up the offending feet, and gently squeeze each one, looking for a flinch reaction that would indicate pain.

✓ While you're at it, check for heat in the front hooves.

✓ Check the digital pulse (that's at the back of the foot just above the hoof) and decide if it's "bounding" (really fast and hard).

✓ Check manure production (it should be normal) and use the stethoscope to listen to her gut. It should be rumbly and squeaky. Silent is bad.

Another vet once told me that a horse has duplicates of everything for a reason. If you're not sure whether a foot is hot, check another one for comparison. If the lung on one side sounds weird, check the other one. Nice of Mother Nature to provide us with a learning experience, isn't it?

Take the time to run through these tests when the horse is well and happy, and you'll be better prepared when the worst happens. Your vet will appreciate all the information you can share, and your horse will benefit from your efforts, I guarantee.

Always look a gift horse in the mouth!

Chapter 24

For Want of a Check, the Horseshoer Was Lost

As if you don't have enough on your plate, your new horse's feet are about to land there next to the asparagus. If, like the novice me, you believe you buy a horse complete with all the necessary add-ons, then, like me, you are going to be surprised when the shoer shows up. Assuming for the sake of assuming that you are boarding your horse somewhere where actual horse care is going on, someone will eventually call the shoer, and you will cross paths with the most exotic and enigmatic of all the horse professionals in your arsenal. I saved him for last so as not to scare you.

If the vet with his "suspensory" this and "hindgut" that hasn't already sent you scurrying to buy an owner's manual, this fine soul will put you over the top. It is in your best interests to ask your vet and your barn owner for recommendations when you are seeking a horseshoer. Relying on your fellow boarders and the few horse people you have managed to accumulate at this point could send you down the rosy path to high-priced corrective shoeing before you can say, "I think my horse would look great in pink Nikes."

Here's the straight story: Your horse has hooves, and they need attention approximately every six weeks. Eight if you're lucky. Four if you're not. If you fell for an equine with fragile, brittle, or damaged feet, you're going to need your farrier's (that's the classy name for horseshoer) number on speed dial.

For my own part, I call my farrier whenever I have a horse with something funny going on anywhere that doesn't actually show evidence of missing chunks of hide. "Two senior citizens walk into a bar…oh, by the way, Pokey's off on the left front" is typical of our conversations. You won't get to the email joke level with your new best friend right away, so here's what you need to know about your horse's feet:

1. He has four. If one looks "funny" to you, compare it to another one on the other side. Remember, that's why nature gave them parts in pairs.

2. Your horse's hoof is the equivalent of the nail on your middle finger. When he does that pawing thing, he really is giving you the finger. Get used to it.

3. Feet grow. Naked feet on hard ground wear down a bit, but not enough. Without regular care, your horse's tootsies will look like Great Aunt Ida's fingernails in a few months. Nasty! Overgrown feet are an obvious sign of neglect.

4. You don't need to know everything about how your horse's feet work, but you should have a general idea. Your shoer will tell you the rest.

5. The line, "No hoof, no horse" isn't a joke.

6. Shoes are not the answer to every problem, but neither is "natural barefoot trim". Your farrier knows best. He went to school for this. You only bought a horse.

7. Whatever he's charging probably isn't enough (unless he's the rare Horseshoer to the Stars who charges extra for bragging rights).

8. Your horse deserves to be pain-free.

9. So does your shoer, so make sure the horse is well-behaved, dry, and clean for his appointment.

10. Once you have found a farrier you like, cherish him and give him expensive gifts.

Okay, maybe that last is a little over the top. My shoer made me say it.

So here we are. You have a horse whose feet were the last thing on your mind, and you are about to find out that your farrier is the most important person in your horse's life. Sorry, Dr. Fazio, but I call Jack more often than I call you.

You can spend long hours talking to various horse people in your area, and no two will agree on what's right for a horse's feet. Hooking up with a shoer requires a certain leap of faith and a willing to commit for at least a few months. The duration of the commitment will depend entirely on how good a job he (or she—though more uncommon, there are many female farriers) does. Any changes you and s/he make to your horse's feet will take as much as a year to finalize (or to recover from).

How can you tell whether your farrier is right for you and your horse? Is your horse sound? Does he head for the next county when he sees the farrier's truck? Do you feel like moving out of town when you see that appointment on your calendar? If you and your horse are comfortable with the farrier and s/he is keeping your horse sound, you got a good one.

There are many, many good farriers. There are also a few who learned their skill via the internet or by watching someone and deciding "Hey! I can do that!" There are professional associations for farriers. You might start by checking the Journeyman Farriers' Association. Henry Heymering is the founder and a great guy to talk to about the world of horseshoeing. He's written books for shoers, and you might do well to check them out.

Of course, not all farriers belong to associations. If there's one thing you can count on in the horse world, it's that horsemen love to share information, whether you want it or not. Put out feelers at some of the big training barns in your area. Ask your vet. Ask at the farms that are successfully breeding and selling horses. Take a poll and make a list. Then just start at the top. Farriers are busy people. There are not nearly enough of them in the world. So the first one (or five) you call may not be able to take you on. Don't take it personally. Just move on.

What does your horse need? Unless you have bought a truly damaged horse (which will not have happened if you bought this book first and read the chapter on the pre-purchase vet exam and remained strong in the face of "soft eyes"), odds are in favor of your horse needing nothing more than a trim or a reset (removal and replacement of the same shoes he was already wearing with a trim to level the feet) every six to eight weeks. The shoer will trim the hoof to keep the foot striking the ground evenly and at an angle that does not conflict with the natural angles of the horse's leg. He may or may not apply a shoe. You will tell him if the horse is having any problems, and he will tell you whether or not your horse needs clips (small points pulled up from a hot metal shoe and bent to hold the shoe more firmly onto the hoof), trailers (elongated ends to the forks of the shoe meant to help the horse strike the ground properly), rolled toes, bars, studs, or any of the other major and minor modifications that can be made to the shoeing process.

The goal is to protect the horse's hoof from damage and keep the hoof and leg in proper alignment to avoid arthritis and other joint and tendon ills. The hoof alone is home to several bones and joints, so this is no small task. Trust your professional, and don't let the farrier be the low man on your bill-paying hierarchy. If you don't pay him, he won't come back.

It is wise for every horse owner to be present for at least most of the shoeing experiences his horse undergoes. You can phone it in, but there's nothing like listening to the shoer explain his craft to make you realize that this animal eating you out of mortgage and cable connection is as complex as that college roommate you ditched because you thought she might be from another planet.

Chapter 25

What We Don't Do With Horses (Especially at a Boarding Farm)

"But he's my horse! You can't tell me what to do with him." Read that aloud in a huffy voice, and you will be wearing the hat of the Boarder We All Hate.

Yes, it's perfectly true that if you own the horse, most of the decisions about what he does and doesn't get to do are yours. Most of them. If you have the horse at home, then you have more leeway. Only the horse will object when you suddenly have a Stupid Attack and do something that falls into the You Should Know Better category. But if you're boarding at someone else's farm, then you have to toe the line or move on. These are a few of the things I've seen done that should not be, ever:

- o Ride the piss out of your horse every Saturday come hell or high water because that's your only day off. The barn manager will deal with his lameness or colic. That's his job.

- o Use mechanical training devices that you don't understand but which you saw in a magazine article (which obviously makes you an expert).

- o Ride your obnoxious, out-of-control, bucking horse in the ring during beginner lessons.

- o Do that and expect the instructor to "help you out" when you finally realize you're about to die.

- o Bathe your horse daily, put bows in its mane, spray it with all sorts of expensive goop, then put it in its stall and leave so the horse's hooves can rot and the farm staff has to figure out what you want done with him.

o   Leave the farm on horseback without telling anyone where you're going. This is especially effective ten minutes prior to any scheduled feeding.

o   Refuse vet care for your horse unless he's "bleeding out the eyes", as one boarder put it. Barn managers love dealing with horses in the throes of complex medical conditions.

o   While you're at it, refuse regular vaccinations, dental care and hoof trims because horses in the wild don't need all that stuff. It's all just a conspiracy among equine professionals who want to get rich off your horse. If another horse in the barn gets sick or yours requires extra care, that's not your problem.

o   Let your horse become dangerously spoiled and do nothing to correct his behavior so the other boarders and the barn staff have to draw straws to see who gets stuck dealing with him or stalled next to him.

o   Bring in your "friend who used to have a horse" to work on training your animal without clearing it with the barn manager and possibly the insurance company first.

o   Adhere to the latest in horse whispering techniques and insist that everyone who handles your horse also whisper to him even when he's eating their clothing.

o   Make endless excuses for your horse's quirks instead of finding professional help for him.

o   Do not bother to read any of the horse-related magazines, books or websites, so you can't identify any problem that might arise or have any clue at all as to what is and is not appropriate management for your horse. Panic is always fun around the barn.

o Decide for yourself where your horse should be turned out and turn him out there without consulting the barn staff or engaging your own brain sufficiently to recognize that this might cause a problem.

o Buy a bag of sweet feed, corn, or oats, and feed your horse bucketsful as a treat. Be surprised when he colics or loses his mind.

o Beat your horse, publicly or in private, because he "needs it".

o Ride drunk or drugged. Your fellow boarders just love a quick run to the ER to save your sorry butt.

There are more, but listing them is depressing. Forty-eight years around horses has shown me that many owners should be tried and punished for their ability to ignore the obvious and go blithely about the destruction of a lovely animal and the sanity of the staff charged with caring for it.

I can hear you thinking, "But Fluffernutter really does need to be beaten for his own good! And I only have one day to ride. He loves his bucket of oats after a hard workout. You can't tell me I'm wrong, because the horse is doing fine."

Yes, I can, and no, he's not. You are just too naïve to realize that there's a problem. If you are reading this book, then you are probably a first-time horse owner. You need to be at least up to horse number three to have any idea of just how bad things might be for your equine buddy.

This is coming straight from the horse's mouth. Lest you forget, I'm the brilliant equestrian who thought she'd killed her first horse because with ten plus years of riding and showing experience, she still couldn't tell death from sleep. Nor could she figure out that a horse that hadn't been ridden for six years could in no way tolerate daily rides of an hour or more without some sort of body-building exercises first.

As for the "pro's" out there who have been raised in a show barn where horses seem to be magically groomed and tacked-up and care isn't an issue, I know some of you, too. I remember in particular one world-class rider from whom I took a lesson or two and who could not begin to tell me whether my tack fit the horse or whether the horse was far enough along in training to do what I was asking her to do. He could ride, and he could teach riding, but he didn't know much about horses. Not someone to rely on for management advice. And I know one who did permanent damage to a client's horse and called it a "learning experience" for his personal edification. If the shiny boots fit, take another look in the mirror and see if you can't find one last functioning brain cell that can stand some lessons in horse management and training.

You, as Horse Owner, do have rights. You have the right to be responsible for every bad thing you teach your horse and everything you do that injures or sickens him. Exercise those rights and the right to be a good caretaker for an animal who wasn't given a choice about where his next meal is coming from.

You can't put a price on the joy of a good relationship.

Afterword:

Happy Harriet Horseperson Lives!

If after all of this you still own a horse, you have an excellent opportunity ahead for learning and teaching on both sides of the fence. Discouragement is part of the game. So are confusion and frustration, excitement and moments of pure joy. Expense, of course, is a given, and may loom largest in your mind.

However you approach your life with horses, remember this: You chose this path, but your feet are not bound to a single direction. You have the ability to learn and grow and change the path as you go. Eventually you will find a way with your horse that makes both of you happy and keeps you out of both the poorhouse and the asylum.

But however long and complex your quest may be, never give up the opportunity for the pleasure that comes with even a questionable relationship with a non-human mind. If you are open to it, you will see things through your horse's eyes that you never expected. Let the moment be and live it thoroughly. No matter how badly you may have made your approach to this particular lifestyle change, you can ride through it to a whole new horizon.

Be brave. Be bold. Be open. Get medication when necessary. Your horse life awaits!

Printed in the United States
by Baker & Taylor Publisher Services